I0621952

In Faith, I Thrive
Sylvia Worsham

Sulit Press

Copyright © 2024 by Sylvia Worsham.

All rights reserved.

No portion of this book may be reproduced in any form without written per-mission from the publisher or author, except as permitted by U.S. copyright law.

Paperback: 979-8-9905753-2-5

Ebook: 979-8-9905753-1-8

Edited by Alyssa Rabil and Michelle Savage

Cover art by Christy Jaynes

Sulit Press

www.sulitpress.com

Dedication

For my heroes, Dad and Aunt Patricia

Thank you for embodying perseverance and purpose. Because of your beautiful example, I stayed true to my divine purpose and became the woman God envisioned me to be. I love you.

Contents

Introduction

Dear Light Bringers:

When God prompted me to write the first version of this book, *Journey To Me*, I was outside of a movie theater in Dallas, Texas in 2010. My three girlfriends and I had spent the last two and half hours, laughing, and crying while watching *Eat, Pray, Love,* starring Julia Roberts. She portrayed Elizabeth Gilbert, a woman in the throes of spiritual warfare after her divorce who chronicled her journey to love and happiness. A persistent thought emerged, "Write the Hispanic version of *Eat, Pray, Love.*"

Like Gilbert, I faced a significant **Turning Point** in my life, my first marriage crumbled, and I found myself in a profound spiritual transformation. My relationship with God was in the primitive stages. I believed in Him but did not trust Him to guide me. As a child, I attended Catholic church and school but did not know how to pray or have a relationship with Him. I relied heavily on my own understanding. Surrender and acceptance of God's will were foreign concepts to me. In those years, my fear called the shots in my life. I needed to stay in control of my circumstances. So, instead of listening and acting on God's guidance, I chose to ignore His prompting.

It would take me ten years and three miracles within seventy-two hours to surrender thoughts like, *What can I offer the world*? and *Who am I to guide others*? and act on His prompting to write and publish *Journey to Me: Trust the Wisdom of Change.* By then, I learned to align myself with God's master plan for my life.

God taught me lessons along the way which I share with you here. Once I released my fears and trusted Him to guide me, I began to "see" what He needed me to understand and apply. My path cleared once I stepped out in faith. My journey to my **SOUL** and to joy became the most profound transformation of my life. It led me down the path of **Self-love**, which transformed my relationships with my dad, husband and children. It helped me create win-win situations in my career and make loving choices in other areas of my life.

When I went through my coaching certification with the John Maxwell team in 2017 and learned how to work with my **Subconscious Mind**, I realized I made certain choices in life. John Maxwell is known worldwide as an authority on Leadership concepts and has written over seventy books on the subject. He has a company dedicated to train individuals to be speakers, coaches and trainers on his material, and this is known as the John Maxwell team. It was a deep-dive into this training that made many of the "missing pieces" suddenly make sense. My book is meant to help you understand how your **EGO** (self-image), which is composed of your **Limiting Beliefs**, **Habits**, and patterns of behavior, can sabotage you. You'll read about the amazing capabilities of your two minds, the **Subconscious** and **Conscious**, and how to learn to work with your **Subconscious Mind** so it works in your favor. I've included information on behavioral patterns created by your **Subconscious Mind** to protect you, and about the Five Cycles of Transformation, my own guide to becoming "one" with my **EGO**, **SOUL**, and **Spirit**.

During Covid I felt a "push" from God to compile the stories into the book you hold in your hands today. Through His guidance, I emerged from the darkness of fear-driven beliefs, and **Habits** to find my voice, **SOUL**, joy and light. It became a journey of self-discovery in many ways.

Halfway through, I uncovered the woman God created me to be and my divine **SOUL's** purpose.

Turning Points or "shifts" can be life-changing. In this book I share some of the most intimate **Turning Points** of my life in the hope that you'll feel seen, understood and will step into your spiritual gifts and light to become the person you were born to be.

Since becoming a certified coach and speaker, I've helped professional women who are experiencing a deep spiritual change or are at a crossroads, to break free from their fear-based beliefs, allow more joy into their lives, and build a trusting relationship with God. My book is used to conduct three masterminds all building on each other. The first one titled Freedom from Fear helps women empower their **EGO** (self-image) from doubt to confidence. The second one, Joy in the Journey, guides them to discover their authentic **SOUL** selves and shift their motivation from fear to joy. The last one, Trust in God's Sovereignty, guides them to surrender their daily worries to God and align with God's master plan for their life.

Even though I use scripture in the book, I don't consider myself a religious or Christian coach. I am a faith-based coach because I guide towards a relationship with God.

My **Desire** for you is that you will experience more faith and trust while navigating transitions in life. I want you to know unequivocally how strong, courageous, and empowered you are.

The answers you seek and the code to your success are inside of you. My hope is that you will live in joy and step into your divine purpose so your light shines brightly.

Many blessings,

Sylvia

Chapter 1
I Am Responsible

Traumatic memories create feelings, patterns of behavior, and **Limiting Beliefs** steering your choices in life. As kids, we often traveled to Mexico City to visit my mom's family during the summers. My parents wanted to ensure they raised us proud of our Mexican heritage. July and August, we spent trekking across the mountain sides, exploring the historical significance of our culture, tasting delicacies, and swimming in the Riviera Maya.

Daddy grew up in a highly abusive home, in Monterrey, Mexico. His father lived as a raging alcoholic, and an emotional, physical, and mental abuser who beat up his mom in front of the seven children. Dad begged his mom to leave him after he witnessed the cruel and evil way he kicked a sore on her foot.

My grandmother begged him, "Please José, anywhere else but don't kick me there!" as she lay on the floor of their home in a fetal position waiting for the next blow.

When I inquired why he beat them up, Dad responded, "Any stupid little thing would set him off. During those years in Mexico, men believed they were superior to women. If she didn't cook it just the way he liked it, if she failed to iron his clothes the way he wanted them, he would hit her."

School became a struggle for Dad as he coped with the abuse he received from his father and older siblings. At a young age, he took refuge at his maternal aunt's home, Maria, or La Muñeca, "the doll," as everyone lovingly called her. She worked as the head of the accounting department at the most profitable brewery in Monterrey in 1950. She took her responsibility seriously for her family, She never married and raised my father on her own. Because of her love, dedication, and money, she made my dad the responsible and successful man he is today.

In October, 1961, my parents met at a dance. They were twenty-one-years old. It was the annual dance of the Universidad Autónoma de Nuevo León for Engineers. My Uncle Juan José, a recent graduate of chemical engineering school, took Mom as his date. She vividly recalls how her older brother twirled her around the floor of a grand ballroom where two orchestras were playing tandas (a set of five songs) that the couples danced to continuously. A couple of tandas into the dance, an architectural student and a phenomenal dancer, shorter than her with a spit-fire personality, invited her to dance. After a few turns around, she spotted a handsome dark-haired man who seemed to follow them around the dance hall.

"He would stare at me with those dark, brown, intense eyes," she remembers. He wore a brown suit with a mustard-colored long-sleeve shirt and a tie.

Her brother, Juan, tapped her on the shoulder and said, "Chaparrita (his pet name for my mom) nos vamos después de esta tanda!" (Shorty, we are leaving after the next song).

She returned to their table where his friends and their dates sat. One girl informed her, "Your brother is off with a girl he just met. I don't think you are leaving just yet."

Mom Chased Me!

Although beautiful, her crystal clear heels, a gift from her dad from a recent trip to Mexico City, were killing her! She gladly sat down to join her brothers' colleagues. The water in front of her invited a much-needed refreshment.

Then she felt a presence above her as a hand extended toward her "Bailamos?" which in English translates to "Shall we dance?" His voice was deep and confident. Mom's green eyes met his direct gaze and her heart fluttered. For a moment, time stood absolutely still, her heart pounding out of her chest and legs shaking with anticipation. Her hand rested on her leg to steady herself. She resisted the urge to excitedly say yes to the handsome stranger she bumped into all night on the dance floor. *Who was he?*

In an effort to stay dignified and attractive, she calmly took his hand and said, "Si, gracias." She explained, "In those days we danced close together despite not knowing each other well with our heads lightly touching. Your dad was a phenomenal dancer who knew exactly how to twirl and move you on a dance floor. It felt like we were floating, so effortless and graceful."

Dad recalled this meeting differently. He said, "Mom chased me!" as he flashed a brilliant smile and winked at me.

During the seven years that Dad was at medical school, he spent entire Sundays at my mom's home. My maternal grandfather worked as a chemical engineer with Pemex, the Mexican state-owned petroleum company, and was a jovial man who loved to crack jokes and play the piano. My grandmother, Eva, worked as a traditional homemaker, who prepared lavish meals for her family of nine. Mom remembered the first time Dad met my grandparents. She left him sitting stiffly in the foyer while she went to the kitchen to tell my grandmother he would join them when she heard her dad's boisterous voice say, "Y usted quién es?" which in English translates to "And who are you?"

Grandfather Juan José, impeccably dressed, newly shaved, and showered, ventured out of his bedroom completely unaware of the serious and shy suitor who sat patiently waiting to meet the parents of the girl he dated. Mom rushed back to find Dad as he struggled to make a coherent sentence out.

"I am José Luis, nice to meet you." as he extended his right hand and looked squarely at the man who would one day become his father-in-law.

You Promised We Would See Snow!

My parents married on March 4, 1968. Several years and three kids later, we took a day trip as a family to Popocate-petl, a volcano just outside of Mexico City limits. Daddy woke us up early to travel with our aunts, uncles, and cousins. He promised my brother, sister, and I, we would see snow. We lived in South Texas, "the Valley," which offered heat, humidity, and lows in the fifties. We rarely needed a coat, let alone mittens and earmuffs. Charlie Brown's Christmas special gave us our reference to snow. We knew it would be epic, no doubt. I quickly jumped out of bed despite it being five in the morning, and hastily dressed. My exhilaration succumbed to the bone-chilling feeling as my feet touched the floor. Early mornings at my grandmother's home evoked images of icicles and polar bears. Mom left a fuzzy, snug sweater and socks at arm's length and, with expert agility, I slipped them on as quickly as my seven-year-old self could do it.

After the two-hour drive, we climbed to the summit. The gorgeous day captured my mind and all the details remain so fresh with the radiant blue sky speckled with a few white clouds. Despite the sun being out, it was still chilly, and while the cold weather didn't stop us, the altitude only made us feel the chill more. Our heavy jackets kept us warm with our hands inside our pockets. The crisp air was a fresh change from the Mexico City smog. I felt my lungs strengthen with each sure-footed step up the incline. My eyes focused on the white caps of the dormant volcano and my mind danced delightfully as I imagined all of the activities I would enjoy with the snow. *Will it feel like ice cream? What does it taste like?* I wondered.

Halfway through the climb, a part of the group wanted to descend. The altitude took a toll on our blood pressure and some felt the physical effects. Daddy debated on calling it a day, but I stubbornly put my hands on my hips and reminded him of his promise to see snow. My dad gave in to my demands and a large group of us, which included my two-year-old baby sister, Roxanne (Roxy), continued our climb. My mom descended the mountain, along with a small group of others.

When we finally made it to the summit, my sister, and a couple of older cousins and uncles played with the snow until our fingers were raw and frigid. The first thing I did was put snow in my mouth! I couldn't resist tasting it. My cousin responded in disgust. "Eww Sylvia, what are you doing? Do you know how dirty it is? Yuck."

"It tastes like water." I wisely informed him of my experiment.

Roxy busily made snowballs to throw. She had a twinkle of mischief in those light green eyes of hers as her small hands attempted to make the biggest snowball. I smiled inwardly and created one myself to throw at my Uncle Hector, who stood nearby. He was a twenty-year-old who acted more like a big kid. His smile lit up a room in a good-humored way and brightened our days. We loved our mornings with him; he sang along as Journey and Heart blasted on the speakers. My mind snapped back to the cold reality of my thoughts when I felt a splash of powder and water hit me in the face, a perfect hit from Hector who laughed heartily and said "Gotcha!" I turned around to see both rascals and their loot of snowballs waiting on me to shoot back. *Doomed*, I thought as I quickly assembled my stash.

If She Dies, It's Your Fault!

On the way back down, Roxy put her hands in the pockets of her jacket while running to catch up with Dad who was not far ahead of us. As she toddled down the hill, her feet became tangled and before we knew it she rolled down and hit her head on a rock, giving her a cut just above her left eye. A fountain of blood exploded around her and covered her light blue jacket on both sides, her golden curls now soaked red. The sound of her piercing cries carried down the summit. I ran at sonic speed towards her. Terror choked me as my breath rapidly increased. Dad rushed to Roxy's side and our family formed a protective circle around her.

Dad, with his training in medical school, and Vietnam as a surgeon, knew all too well that the effects of altitude coupled with my sister's age, created a recipe for disaster. If she fell asleep, she may never wake up. Fear and anxiety gripped him, and his face did not conceal his terror. He turned angrily in my direction and said, "If your sister dies, it will be your fault." He said that because I insisted we continue our ascent to the summit. I sat stunned and petrified all at once. No one came to me afterward to comfort or tell me Dad lashed out because he was afraid of losing my sister. Our carefree day of playing in the snow abruptly ended as we rushed down the mountain to take Roxy to a nearby hospital. My seven-year-old mind couldn't comprehend the thought of losing my little sister. The next memory to come to me, as I recall the events of that awful day, is of me praying to God to let my baby sister live during the ride to the hospital. All the while, we heard my mom's loud sobs as the van sped down the highway.

Even at that young age, the thoughts running through my mind were, *Why had I been so stubborn? This is my fault! If I had not insisted, this wouldn't have happened! Am I stupid? What was I thinking? I should've known the dangers.*

I Did Not Survive

This traumatic moment marked a **Turning Point** in my young life and unfortunately, it also created a **Limiting Belief**, *I am not trustworthy to make the right decisions in life.*

Everyone experiences **Turning Points** in their lives. A **Turning Point** is otherwise known as a time of transition or crossroads. Examples include divorce, a change in careers, a near-death experience, loss of a loved one etc.

These changes can be intimidating because they can deplete your confidence and can take time to process. But they can also be seen as a divine intervention meant to guide you to your **SOUL's** path. In crossroads like these, you will face choices. You can choose to take a leap of faith, learn from this experience and take a different course of action or you may fall into the **EGO** trap and avoid your pain by letting your beliefs keep you from moving forward.

The Turning Point leads to the creation of patterns of behavior and Limiting Beliefs which attach themselves to a feeling. At the moment of trauma, your emotional mind, otherwise known as the **Subconscious Mind**, will store the feeling you experienced and attach it to the **Pattern of Behavior** in its attempt to protect you from feeling pain. In my case, after experiencing the trauma of my sister's accident, my **Subconscious Mind** created a control **Pattern of Behavior** and attached it to my feeling of doubt. Anytime doubt showed up in my life, my mind recalled this pattern of control and acted on my behalf automatically. Put another way, my feeling of doubt directed my reaction of staying in control of circumstances and formed an attachment to it. I programmed my mind to react in this way. Any time doubt showed up in other areas of my life, (relationships, career, finance), my mind instinctively responded with control. A relatable example of this is feeling doubtful about the financial market and not knowing whether to invest in the stock market or keep your money in the bank. If you programmed your mind to respond with control when doubt is present you'll keep your money in the bank because it is safer than investing it and potentially losing it. When different circumstances arise in your life, and the original feeling is present, the **Subconscious Mind** will know how to respond to it in the way your mind has been programmed. This automatic response that emanates from your **Subconscious Mind** is called a **Trigger**.

Being blamed for my sister's accident changed my relationship with my siblings forever. I took on parental responsibility. Even though my sister survived, part of me had not.

The mind is powerful, especially the **Subconscious Mind**. It has zero ability to accept or reject information, in other words, it is literal. When these significant emotional events or traumas occur, your mind will form beliefs. In coaching, the term is **Limiting Beliefs**, because they limit your amazing capability as a human being and are fear-based.

It took years for my **Conscious Mind** to gain the **Awareness** of the **Limiting Belief** which buried itself deeply into my **Subconscious Mind**. Anytime the feeling of distrust/doubt showed up in my life, it surfaced and wreaked havoc. The worst part, I functioned completely unaware of its existence. I simply reacted to the situation.

The key component in moving past this incident in my life involved me accepting that my programming came from this traumatic event. I also accepted I did not know the complete story or the extent of abuse my dad experienced as a child. Anger served as an automatic response his **Subconscious Mind** created in response to fear. His family abuse modeled this to him as a young boy. Once I accepted it, I then understood why he responded as he did. Finally, I appreciated the lesson this experience taught me. Only then could I forgive myself and my father. My father did the best he could, based on his conscious **Awareness** at the time, which now as a coach I realize, is limited to our choices and thoughts. The deepest part of your mind, the subconscious part, is truly in control. It runs on automatic. Until you learn about the power of this mind, you don't realize it is in control. You "think" you are in control.

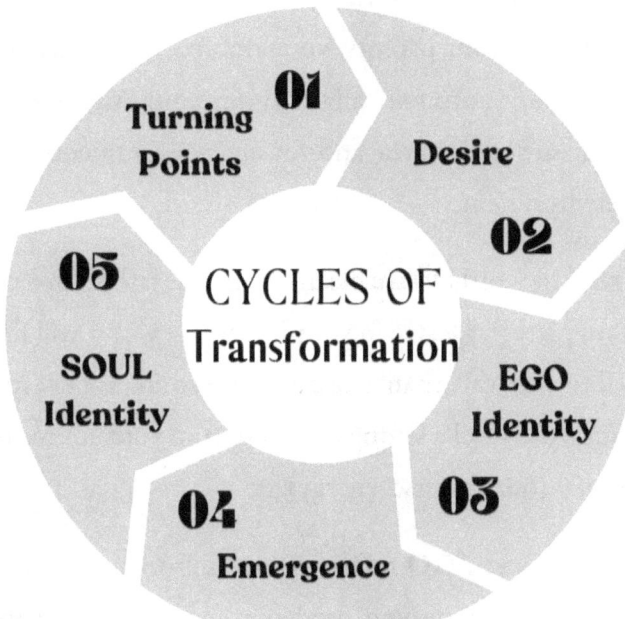

Most of this book focuses on sharing my personal stories and experiences as a way to illustrate how I came to find joy by learning to trust God. Since I also want you to be able to directly apply these learnings to your own life, I'll be referring to the following key terms and concepts throughout this book. These terms are ones I discovered as I journeyed from fear to my divine purpose and are the blueprint I used to use change as a catalyst of my spiritual transformation.

Turning Points or Life Pivotal Moments: are marked by a period of reflection where choices are considered.

Your programming (**Limiting Beliefs**, the modeling you received from your parents, your trauma, etc) is driving your decisions automatically without your **Awareness**. Emotions are raw and real and you are easily influenced by your environment.

Desire: The word **Desire** means "from the father," meaning God places a **Desire** in your heart to act. You will feel excited to start this change because everything is new and exciting. You'll feel a strong connection to your source of wisdom, (God, universe, energy).

EGO Identity: EGO refers to your self-image. It consists of your programming, modeling you received in your childhood, trauma, and **Limiting Beliefs** which will be in control of your actions during this phase in the cycle. This is the self that interacts with the outside world, the one influenced by your environment which can negatively impact your spiritual and emotional growth. In this third phase, your **Subconscious Mind** rejects any new change you attempt by testing your resolve. There will likely be a disconnect from your inner source of wisdom/God. Confidence, competence are low and doubt will reign your thoughts.

Emergence: It is marked by momentum, transformation, **Awareness**, and faith. **Desire** is strong to continue the path towards change. Results are visible and empower you to continue moving forward. You will confidently act on the promptings you receive from God/**Intuition**/source of wisdom. Through your consistency and effort, you push past your old **EGO** (self) to emerge into your **SOUL Identity**.

SOUL Identity: Marked by identity, alignment to spirit, joy, and God's master plan. Your **Subconscious Mind** accepts a new identity and automatically operates on new programming. Alignment to God/inner source of wisdom is strong. You confidently and competently align to the **SOUL's** vision. You turn towards your inner voice/spirit/God when you make life pivotal decisions.

The Power of the Two Minds

Conscious Part of Mind: *"Your thinking mind,"* represents 10% of daily activities, and stores your choices, thoughts, self-talk, and attitudes here.*

Subconscious Mind: *"Your emotional mind,"* represents 90% of daily activities, and stores memories, significant emotional events, traumas,* **Limiting Beliefs,** *feelings,* **Reactions,** **Habits,** *patterns of behavior, and triggers here.*

The Seven Patterns of Behavior

Patterns of behavior operate at a subconscious level and protect you from feeling pain. They are recurrent ways of behaving that form attachments to feelings.

Achiever: a **Pattern of Behavior** characterized by feelings of unworthiness. This pattern is characterized by a need to achieve in order to feel happy, and gain recognition and acceptance from success. An example of this showing up in your life is: You are president of a networking group and are put in charge of an event. You will work yourself to the point of exhaustion to ensure its success and will delegate very little of the responsibility to others.

Avoider: a **Pattern of Behavior** characterized by feelings of being overwhelmed. This behavior escapes into a flurry of activity to avoid pain. Examples of the **Avoider** pattern showing up in your life are: You've lost your mom recently and are in deep grief. You schedule one house project after another to avoid feeling the loss.

Distractor: characterized by a lack of motivation and being stuck in a rut. An example of this is you are an entrepreneur and you've had setbacks. You will do busy work but nothing that truly moves the needle forward in your business.

Perfectionist: characterized by two identities, the internal and the one you want people to see. They lack **Self-love**. An example of a **Perfectionist** pattern showing up in your life is when you beat yourself up after you make a mistake. Failure is not an option for you.

Security Seeker: characterized by fear and paralysis when change is present. People with this pattern need certainty and will seek comfort in their misery because it's terrifying to grow. An example of this pattern in your life is fighting for control in arguments with others or staying in a horrible relationship because you fear the unknown.

Succeeder: characterized by inconsistency and lack of follow-through. People with this pattern are always looking for the next big thing. Examples of this showing up in your life are: It's a new year and you sign up for a gym membership. You have the intention of sticking with it but a month into it once the excitement of the change dies down you stop going and quit altogether.

Victim: characterized by lack of responsibility for their role in situations. It's always someone else's fault. An example of this pattern showing up in your life is: Your spouse travels for work. The **Victim** picks a fight before they leave and will refuse to take ownership for their role in the fighting but will blame their travel on the lack of connection in the marriage. "If only my husband or wife would stay home then our marriage would be solid," is how the **Victim** rationalizes the fight.

My Security Blanket

One reason the **Subconscious Mind** will solidify traumas or significant emotional events and create beliefs about them is to protect you at the moment from feeling hurt. However, over a span of time it can contribute to keeping you stuck in your circumstances, like it did for me. I perpetuated an angry identity for about thirty-six years. To protect me, my **Subconscious Mind** created a **pattern of behavior**, the **Security Seeker** pattern which attached itself to a feeling of control and security. Any time this feeling showed up later in life, I would become fearful and paralyzed. I fought for control in arguments with others. I stayed in my box, fearful of change.

It made sense for my seven-year-old mind to form a bubble of security when it happened, but as time wore on, it prevented my creative and fun spirit from emerging. It found comfort being the responsible and serious sibling, but it robbed me of the joy in life. When I became a mother to my first-born, I failed to relate, I didn't know how to play or have fun.

From the coaching perspective, this incident on the mountain played a role in destroying my capacity to identify with kids my age. I aged overnight and never fit in with my peers. Now it makes sense. My father's fears triggered his anger at this traumatic event. Any significant, fear-based emotional events and memories he recalled on automatic. He was completely unaware of these memories, and he had no conscious control of his emotions. His **Subconscious Mind** controlled his **Reactions**. This is how the mind works. Scary, isn't it?

For years, my parents could not understand the reason behind my anger and why I treated my siblings as if they were my children. They chalked it up to me being a typical teenager, hormonal and temperamental. Turns out there was a deep wound needing restoration.

A Valuable Lesson

At twenty-one-years-old, and after years in therapy, my dad made a comment about the incident triggering an angry response from me. Suddenly I understood the reason for my anger. It was the biggest "Aha" moment of my young life. The memory unlocked with his comment. My therapist explained to me when my dad yelled at me on the summit, he inadvertently transferred his parental responsibilities onto me.

Well, now it makes sense, I thought as she told me. It's as if all the pieces in my mind finally fell into place. It's called **Awareness**. This information made its way from my subconscious to my **Conscious Mind** where now my logic could come into play and I could incorporate my "thinking mind" and forgive my dad for his automatic response. Forgiveness played a huge part in my healing and it can for you, too.

Why was this **Turning Point** life-changing for me? It taught me a valuable lesson in responsibility. I am grateful to my dad for this experience, as painful as it was at the time. Being a responsible teenager guided me to stay clear of drugs or drinking excessively. It kept me straight on my path as a college student. I made good grades, volunteered, and created a nonprofit program to help countless elementary school children.

Responsibility kept me on the track of taking ownership for my role in other highly emotional events like this one, my relationships with others flourished. It guided me in doing the right thing, even when it was challenging to do.

It's one of the values I identify with, and it has become a superpower of mine. In fact, when I worked in sales, being responsible and accountable became major strengths for me, which led me to become an award winning representative. Modeling responsibility to my kids helps shape the beautiful **SOULs** they are becoming in life and will undoubtedly impact their personal and professional lives positively.

Overall, I benefited from the lessons of this amazing **Turning Point**. Pain can transform into something beautiful.

Scripture for Journaling, Meditation, or Prayer

Genesis 3: 1-12 - *Reflect on Adam's failure to communicate to Eve about the Tree of Life (she wasn't there when God told Adam not to eat from the tree)*

Adam failed to take ownership of his role in eating from the tree. Think of a time when you failed to take responsibility for your role in a situation. How did it affect your relationship to others?

Chapter 2
I Am Courageous

In my sophomore year of high school, a boy invited me to the homecoming dance. I couldn't wait to tell my mom, my confidante. Kids had bullied me incessantly at school since the ninth grade, so this was a social win. Mean girls, a group of four, would often make comments about my personal appearance, exclude me from sitting with them at lunch, and ridicule and laugh at me when I participated in French class. I was a solid student in languages and humanities which threatened the leader of this group, who had the second highest GPA in school. Anytime I got a higher grade or was awarded anything from the teachers, she would try to discredit me or question why I received it and she had not.

I was someone who strived for excellence in everything I did and portrayed an inner confidence that others craved which likely triggered their insecurities in them. I wasn't afraid to be myself or speak up during classroom discussions and that bothered them. In sports, I had tenacity and never gave up until the game was over. I gave it my all. This is what led them to bully me. The painful part of it was how Irma, a girl I considered my best friend up until that year, joined in on the daily ritual of taunting and criticizing me. In PE class, I would be teamed up with some of these girls. When I made a mistake on the field, like not catching the ball or not throwing it in time, they would jeer at me, by saying, "Oh look Sylvia can't do it, because she's afraid of breaking or messing up her nails!" It seemed like they were always on alert when I made mistakes or perceived failures and were ready to offer up a ridiculing comment.

Another time, we were put in groups of five in our eleventh grade writing class. Our teacher, Cynthia Pierce, assigned us the project to help the class understand the different parts of writing a piece: introduction, body, and conclusion, by doing it in a creative and visual way. One of the girls who hung around these four bullies was in my group. She came up with the idea to have one of the girls (there were three of us) dress for a date in front of class to showcase the process in writing. The girl was to arrive only wearing a leotard and bring the dress, accessories, makeup to class. The introduction which sets the theme would be the leotard, the outfit would represent the body and the shoes, and accessories would represent the conclusion. She felt too embarrassed to do it, so another girl volunteered. Unfortunately, the volunteer got into a car accident a day before the presentation and could not do it, so I stepped up to present.

I dressed in a leotard and wore a long black coat over it that morning. I stood up in class and despite the astonishment in their faces and the loud whispers I heard some of the girls say, "She thinks her body is hot," and, "Who does she think she is?"

I proceeded to dress in class. I kept my poise and dignity. Afterwards, our group won first place and Mrs. Pierce gave me the highest grade in class. The girl, who came up with the idea, never had the courage to say it was her idea. She led everyone to believe that I had done it for attention. There were times I didn't want to go to school because I dreaded the feeling of inadequacy I often felt at the hands of these four.

I asked Irma once, "Why did you turn on me?"

With very little empathy in her voice and shrug of her broad shoulders, she responded, "I wanted to be popular." This was the greatest betrayal for a girl my age to endure. Mom became my one true friend, and someone I relied on countless times in dealing with all the emotional, mental, and physical cruelties I experienced at school.

So, when a boy invited me to a dance for the first time, I excitedly told my mom, "Guess what?"

"What? Tell me." Her eyes lit up with my excitement.

"I was invited to the homecoming dance. Can you believe it?"

Mom's eyes gleamed with joy and she flashed a bright smile. After all, she watched me come home crying for the past year and half and now I was excited about something at school. We made plans to have the perfect dress made for the day. My mom knew a seamstress who could create anything. We went shopping immediately for all the accessories to complement the dress. For the first time, I felt beautiful and included. In a brief moment of bliss, I imagined my date at the door of our home with a corsage, as he scanned my deep purple form-fitting dress and smiled warmly.

For months, I floated through the hallways at school. Everyone could see my smile from across the room. My confidence grew a little more each day. People noticed and wondered about my aura of happiness. I didn't notice or care when they made fun of me and that made them wonder why I felt so happy. It had been a year of sheer torture. My safe places included home with my mom and a couple of classrooms with my teachers. I didn't let the bullies see they bothered me, but deep down my self-esteem crumbled from the weight of the torture.

You Will Never Belong

My dream of being accepted by the other kids came crashing down two days before the dance. The boy approached me at school during lunch to let me know he couldn't take me to the dance because he needed to see his sick grandmother, but the coward didn't tell me the truth. He asked another girl to the dance. *I had been his second choice*. The drive to be number one from then on was strong. I could feel everyone's eyes on me as he told me the story, and despite my **Desire** to yell at him and call him a liar, I held it together all day. It took every bit of strength to keep from crying. The ugly step-sisters were cackling at me in my mind as my heart ripped into a million little pieces. My pulse quickened and my breath became shallow. I put on the mask of sympathy and understanding. I refused to let anyone see my crushed spirit, especially the boy. I waited all day to sob and the minute I stepped into my mom's car I opened the floodgates.

The entire school knew he asked another girl to the dance. He gave the girls another way to make fun of me. Patricia, the main bully who led the charge, mocked me by making fun of my physical appearance, the way I caught the ball in softball, and she'd make faces when our French teacher asked me to read out loud. She called me ugly and would say, "You see, Sylvia, you were always his second choice. Did you really believe you were one of us? You will never belong. Give up and leave the school. You are not wanted here."

My mom knew Patricia's family. Her father left them for another woman. She felt humiliated and lashed out at weaker kids to feel better about her own situation. Deep down she lacked self-worth despite her brash display of confidence. The hardest part for me was to accept the illusion people held about her, especially the administrators at our Catholic High School. They deemed her a leader because of her high grades and achievements.

Now, as a mom of a teenager, I can't imagine the anguish and anger my mom felt watching her "beautiful daughter" believe she was "too ugly" for someone to take her to a dance. Despite my mom's best efforts to encourage me otherwise, I grew up veiled by this misconception. She begged me repeatedly to transfer to another school, but I stood my ground to not let others defeat me.

She allowed me to cry and yell it all out. Then she told me as gently as she could that I had two choices to make, "Sylvia, you can either go to the dance and have the time of your life, or you can stay home and become their **Victim**. Either way, I love you and am proud of you."

I sat there with tears covering my face, thought about what she said, and decided I wanted to have fun. It would be a shame not to show off my beautiful dress. My mom already thought of calling a good friend of hers to ask if her son could take me to the dance. Danny was four years older than me and had a girlfriend. His mom explained to him the situation, and he talked to his girlfriend. She agreed he needed to help me face my bullies.

The morning of the dance, I awoke to clammy hands and sweat pouring down my back. *Would I have the courage to face them? Would I regret this choice?* I felt nauseous and barely ate all day. As I put on the deep purple satin cocktail dress, my hands lightly shook as I struggled with the zipper. I took a couple of deep breaths to regain my composure and kept my hands steady as I readied myself for the dance. I looked in my mirror and affirmed in a powerful voice, "I am beautiful."

I looked in the mirror as I sprayed the *Aqua Net* in my hair to keep my bangs up all night. I waited by the door until Danny walked up to ring the doorbell, then took a deep breath and opened it. With a smile as wide as possible, I told him how grateful I was to him and his girlfriend for agreeing to take me to the dance.

He grinned, "Sylvia, get ready to have the time of your life!"

We danced and laughed throughout the entire event, and I enjoyed the perfect date all night. Everyone wondered who brought me. To become the talk of the night felt good. Their bewildered eyes as we walked into the ballroom spoke volumes about the thoughts roaming in their minds. *Who is the mystery date? Wow, she came! She's got guts!* I simply glowed.

I Am Ugly!

As we made our way to have our picture taken, we ran into the boy who was originally my date and his first choice. Can you believe I even asked him how his grandmother was doing? I took great pleasure in watching him struggle to answer the question.

Being dumped two days before the dance and lied to, created a belief of *"I am his second choice."* My **Subconscious Mind** buried this belief deep inside of me and would recall it when other women showed up in my love relationships with men. The bullying during my high school years created another **Limiting Belief** of *"I am ugly."* The more they beat me down, the more I believed the lie "*I am ugly.*" I knew it felt real and with each insult this darkness grew inside of me. This type of programming happens when the **Subconscious Mind** lacks the ability to reject the information it receives and keeps us stuck in our circumstances. It's important you choose to stay in environments to empower you rather than beat you down. Now, I completely understand my mother's instinct for me to change schools.

Even though I ignored their comments and stood my ground, my focus became negative towards myself, and my **Subconscious Mind** adopted a **Victim** Mentality Behavioral Pattern which protected me during those years, however, it sabotaged my relationships with others and myself. Your focus will guide the behaviors you choose to adopt in life.

When someone called me pretty or beautiful, I snickered, "Yeah right." I believed deep down I was not beautiful enough to be asked again is something I lived with—all because I *thought* I was ugly.

A Lesson in Courage

When I went through my coaching certification with the John Maxwell team in 2017 and understood how to work with my **Subconscious Mind**, I realized that I made certain choices in life. Many of the "missing pieces' suddenly made sense. I didn't realize at the root of those choices, were my beliefs. As I sat listening to Paul Martinelli, the President of the John Maxwell companies, detail his bullying days and how it led to his **Limiting Belief** of "I am stupid," which influenced his choice of dropping out of school, I suddenly realized how how my **Limiting Belief,** of "I am ugly," steered me to make emotional decisions. Despite the painful choices I made, I am grateful for this amazing **Turning Point** in my life because it taught me a lesson in courage. I faced my fears in a powerful way by going to the homecoming dance and speaking to my bullies. I stood up for myself and the lesson helped shape the woman I became years later. Because of courage I stepped into uncertainty, resulting in some of the most amazing life-altering experiences.

Scripture for Journaling, Meditation, or Prayer

Proverbs 31:25 *She is clothed with strength and dignity; she can laugh at the days to come.*

Reflect on a time when you displayed courage in a situation that breached your dignity. What did you learn about yourself from the courage you displayed?

Chapter 3
I Am Intuitive

When I learned to trust in God's voice and promptings, I began manifesting what I wanted in life. My **Intuition**—my inner voice and wisdom—developed with each **Turning Point**. My sixth sense, and a feeling I got about situations and people helped me make the choice that aligned to my **SOUL** in this next chapter in life.

In my senior year of high school, I visited colleges to see which one suited my goals and personality the best. My amazing English teacher, Mrs. Jan Johnson, suggested I visit Austin College (AC) in Sherman, Texas, a twelve-hour drive from my home. Mrs. Johnson played many roles in my life, first as my favorite teacher and then as my confidant at school. Her classroom provided me with a safe haven during my senior year in high school by offering friendship, guidance, and love. We conversed for hours after school while she graded papers. I would confide in her my fears, joys, and everything happening in my world. She listened patiently and offered excellent advice. Throughout my life, her advice roared into my consciousness when I felt stuck or indecisive. She unleashed the power of my **SOUL**.

My creativity emerged in her classroom throughout my senior year. My writing improved under her tutelage. She helped me tap into the vulnerable parts of my heart to write about painful experiences and how they shaped me. In essence, she encouraged me to tap into my genius. As my English teacher, she saw my gift of writing and encouraged me to use it for my college applications. This empowered me to step into my strengths. She guided my writings and looked over my college essay for AC. In the course of the year, she came to know me well and thought AC would be a compatible fit for me. It would provide me with a smaller community where I would thrive. She was spot on. I fell in love with AC the weekend I went with my mom and was thrilled when I received my acceptance letter. AC ranked as one of the top private colleges in Texas.

Mom remembers dropping me off at college, and tells the story often, always with tears in her eyes. As she left, I happily told her goodbye and ran into my new home. I surprised her with the confidence and joy I displayed as I ran up the steps leading to my dorm room. Then she cried, tears of sadness and pride, the twelve-hour drive home alone.

My new home provided me with simplicity, friendships, and challenges which helped me thrive in my new academic surroundings. Groups like Los Amigos and Service Station gave me a reason to put my activism to work, something I began in high school which brought significant joy to my young life. After school, I volunteered at the local nursing homes to read and visit with their residents. The residents enjoyed having a young person come and visit them and I received the gift of love made visible. During the summers, I volunteered at a pro-bono legal firm that took on asylum cases. I used my fluency in Spanish to help the lawyers communicate with their clients by serving as a legal translator. It made me feel good knowing that I impacted the lives of those fleeing from governments that threatened their safety.

In the groups I met a college recruiter, Rick. We hung out often and before we knew it we fell hard and fast for each other. However, employees of AC were not allowed to date students. We kept it secret for a couple of months until it became evident to everyone that we had mutual feelings for each other. My volunteer work and active participation in community events earned me the respect of the faculty and staff, which made it easier for us to date.

Red Flags Ignored

During the first year at AC, I volunteered at the local high school where the teachers struggled with helping Hispanic kids assimilate into the school system. I noticed a trend while visiting there. An influx of immigrants arriving in Sherman during recent years forced Hispanic children into the education system without having the proper support of language to help them through school. This created an issue of gigantic proportions and Sherman Independent School District (ISD) did not have the staff to manage the situation. I volunteered several times during the week to help, using my fluency in Spanish to help the students, and encourage them to study and graduate from high school. The kids struggled to adapt to the American school system and had difficulty graduating.

During my volunteer work, I created a solution to help Sherman ISD. I immediately recruited Rick to help me formulate a program to help Hispanic kids assimilate and increase their understanding of math and English through experiential learning. The AC Hispanic students became mentors and role models who helped teach the kids math and reading on a weekly basis. AC agreed to let us use their resources on Sunday afternoons. Because of our relationship with the National Hispanic Institute, they agreed to have Generación América, the name we decided on for this mentorship and educational program, under their umbrella of educational programs. It became an overnight success. We were an unstoppable team!

My relationship with Rick grew exponentially during my Sophomore year. We shared a similar drive and purpose and seemed to be a perfect fit. He asked me to marry him and I gladly accepted. Rick had proposed to a couple of girls before me, which did feel like a red flag early on, but as most women know, even though we see the flags, we sometimes choose to ignore them. I just considered myself lucky he chose me. I made an emotional decision instead of a logical one. My **Subconscious Mind** controlled by my **Limiting Belief** of *I am not beautiful and enough* were the drivers of my choice to marry someone who felt unworthy of love too.

Those red flags are something I call **God Instincts**, or **Intuition**. When you make it a daily habit to quiet your mind, you will begin to hear the voice of your **SOUL** and spirit guiding you. You'll see and feel your next steps because your **SOUL** is guiding you instead of your fearful mind with its automatic programming.

Rick flirted with women in front of me. His eyes roamed constantly. He showed me his hand early in our relationship, only I chose to ignore it. My **God Instincts** told me to leave him, but I stayed because of my **Limiting Belief**.

The "gut" or **God Instincts** are there for you to act on them. God knows the timing which benefits you, because he knows your heart and your motivation and those around you too. Often, you choose your way instead of God's way, and create long detours to joy.

During the spring of my sophomore year, I discovered Rick having an affair with a Venezuelan exchange student. Intuitively, I sensed it for months and one night I drove to her apartment only to find his car in her driveway.

My heart sank and tears welled up in my eyes and I screamed, "Why, God? Why would he do this? What did I do to deserve this?" I took a couple of deep breaths and contained the anger, rage, and betrayal I felt in the moment. It was time they owned up to what they were doing.

I debated for several minutes whether I should confront them at all. My heart raced as their entangled bodies in a passionate embrace flashed before my eyes. Rage and disgust filled my entire body as it shook uncontrollably, envisioning them making love. *The evidence sat in front of me this whole time. How did I miss this? I saw the way she hung on his every word and the way his eyes scanned her body.* I walked up the steps slowly, shaking. Shock set in, both legs trembled underneath my jeans, a cold sweat broke out below my cotton blouse and heat flashed underneath my skin. I steadied myself on the railing, afraid I'd faint. The conflicting emotions tied up in a knot and I heard a voice deep inside me say, "End it." For a moment, time stood still, I took a deep breath, and firmly knocked on the door. I shouted, "Cecilia, open the door, I know he is in there."

She opened it with a sly smile on her face, only wearing a shirt. It took every bit of strength to not slap the smug look off her face. In the background, I could see Rick getting dressed. His clothes wrinkled. I looked past her at him and said, "It's over." Then I turned around and walked to my car. He ran after me, trying to stop me from driving away. He even sat in my car, but I boldly told him to let me go and he did.

I sped away from her apartment, and all I remember from the night was calling my mom after I returned to my dorm room. She advised me to leave the dorm so he couldn't find me, and told me to find a safe space to cry it out. I knocked on my good friend Kristi's door and asked her if she could take me somewhere. She called her mom and drove me to her home in East Texas, close to AC. Sobbing the entire way, Kristi listened and gently guided me as she drove. Her voice calmed and reassured me.

All Men Cheat

God sent angels to protect me. I will never forget Kristi's family's kindness to me over the weekend. I needed to be present during Generación América on Sunday, so we drove back early Sunday morning. When I arrived in my dorm room, mutual friends of Rick's and mine and one of the mentors of the program confronted me. She shouted, "How could you do this to Rick?"

"Do what?" I asked her incredulously.

"Nobody knew where you were! He was out of his mind and worried. How dare you scare him like this?"

"How dare I?" I shot back at her. "Do you know what *he* did? I caught him cheating on me Friday night!"

Her face gave way to shock and then what she said astounded me, "All men cheat, but it does not mean he doesn't love you."

I let her know, "I am not the type of woman prepared to take this kind of treatment from a man." Then I grabbed my things quickly and made my way to the auditorium to greet the children and their parents.

Rick tried talking to me, but I simply went on with the program. Eventually he wore me down and my insecurities surfaced. I took him back briefly before he ended things permanently a week before my final exams in the Spring. I practically bombed them all. However, I still managed to pass my courses.

Before I left for the summer, the head of the French department, Dr. Cynthia Manley, approached me to discuss the opportunity to study abroad in Lyon, France, my junior year. In the small community, everyone knew what happened between me and Rick. In fact, most of them knew of his multiple affairs during our relationship. I was the last one to see it. They knew my pain. One in particular, Cynthia knew it all too well. Knowing my potential and not wanting to see me fail because of Rick, she encouraged me to leave AC. I spoke with my parents and filled out the paperwork before I left AC for the summer.

Those first days back home were awful. I spent the first two weeks crying non-stop and staring out the window into my parents' backyard. I spoke no words except to say, "Please, thank you, and good night." Silence dominated.

A Second Chance

Anyone who knows me well will attest, it's not like me to be quiet for so long. My insides were torn and my spirit deflated. Sleep welcomed me with open arms and I gladly accepted the invitation. After two weeks, Mom encouraged me to go out with my friends. As I was walking out the door, the phone rang, and I picked it up to hear Rick. My heart leaped out of my chest. My grandmother, Eva, who spoke to me throughout those two weeks, told me to let him go. Lovingly she reminded me, "Dejalo ir, si regresa fue tuyo, pero si no, nunca fue tuyo." In English it translates to, "Let him go, if he returns, he was yours all along. If he doesn't, he was never yours." She firmly reminded me not to call him and even though I picked up the phone several times, I never did.

When I heard his voice on the other end, I smiled. I told him matter-of-factly I couldn't speak right then.

He complained, "Well I guess I wasn't important to you after all, it seems you have gone on with your life."

"Yes, I have. What do you want?"

"I want a second chance."

Rick asked me to visit his mom, who was recovering from a surgery in Corpus Christi. I asked my roommate Christina to join me on the four-hour drive. It would be the first time I'd be in the same room with him, and I wanted a good friend to be there with me. She agreed to come. A part of me was excited at the possibility of getting back together, and another side of me doubted we would work. *Would I be able to "pretend" everything was okay?* I still loved him, but somewhere deep inside of me I felt wrong about taking him back. My belief system created the problem of "I am not enough." His betrayal bolstered this belief in me.

I Can't Be With Someone Who Cheats

My parents became worried and my dad invited me for a walk on the beach. Dad's voice remained kind and steady throughout. I could tell Mom coached him and no doubt threatened to cut off the protruding parts of his body if he didn't stay calm. She knew all too well his tendency to "control" situations. Now, looking back, I am proud of how he handled himself during our conversation. He simply asked me questions,

"What do you want out of life, Sylvia? Do you believe Rick will make you happy?"

"He's not the man for me, Daddy. I can't be with someone who cheats on me. He's not the one."

I could see the relief on my dad's face. He hugged me and told me I deserved better.

The weekend before I was scheduled to leave the country for my six months abroad, Rick drove down to see me and I took him to the beach to have the "talk" with him. After taking a deep breath, I looked him in the eye to say, "I am not in love with you anymore." Shock and disbelief washed over his face. He looked confused and baffled. My heart raced the whole time I spoke, which felt like hours. I released all my feelings to him, letting him know my heart would not allow him to ever come back again. I stood up for myself, and took my power back, the power I had given to him over and over again. Speaking my truth to him taught me a valuable lesson in **Intuition**. My **Intuition** kicked in several times throughout my courtship, however, my **Limiting Beliefs** kept me from leaving him. Now, I was listening to my inner guidance, my God voice, and felt my strength return.

My broken engagement became instrumental in allowing me to see the power inside of me. The gift of **Intuition** served me well in my life. Since this incident, I have used it to navigate relationships with others, tapping into their energy. It kept me safe abroad, I learned to pay attention to the "signals" and avoided dangerous situations.

Following my God instinct also kept me from making "fearful decisions" in my life. I gave myself the time to allow God to guide my decisions instead of allowing my **Limiting Beliefs** to direct my actions. One clear example happened when I lost a promotion early in my career in sales and, out of spite, wanted to leave. However, a voice interrupted the **Action** to tell me to stay. It persisted throughout a complete day of reflection. Listening to the voice of the Holy Spirit allowed me to make a choice, empowering me. I stayed there and later received the promotion meant for me.

Remember life happens in God's timing, not ours. He wants the absolute best for you, and He knows what must happen first to equip you for those experiences. Instead of living life my way and trying to figure it out, I have relied on my **Intuition** to guide my important choices. God guides me in a powerful way. In fact, his prompting helped me make the decision to become a speaker, coach and author.

Scripture for Journaling, Meditation or Prayer

Psalm 32:8 *I will instruct you and teach you in the way you should go. I will counsel you with my loving eye on you.*

Reflect on a time when you relied on your gut or God instincts. How did it change the course of your life?

Chapter 4
I Am Resilient

L eaving the United States to Lyon, France, two weeks after the fateful conversation with Rick left me feeling exhilarated and terrified all at once. I stepped into uncertainty with my friends and family thousands of miles away. *What would this new chapter bring me? Would I meet new friends? Would my broken heart mend?* These thoughts swirled around my mind during the twelve-hour flight. As soon as I exited the airplane, I took a deep breath and decided to make fun memories over the next six months. Little did I know, this **Turning Point** initiated the cycle of my transformation abroad!

There were six students participating in the exchange program with Austin College and the Université Lumière Lyon II. The program coordinators decided for the first month we would all live with other foreign exchange students in a coed space. Moving from home to college to cohabit with other women had already shocked me. Now,

I would live in the same building with young men! Sharing a bathroom was quite another thing altogether, I'll spare you the frightening details! When you grow up in a traditional Mexican household like mine, prudence takes center stage. My sister and I shared a room. We rarely changed in front of each other, let alone showed skin. Can you imagine the shock of now sharing a *bathroom* with *men* and other women?

France provided me with a new view of the world. The food was decadent, each bite exploded flavor in my mouth and the energy from the French fed my **SOUL**. They soaked up life in their daily interactions. Flower stands decorated each corner, families played in the park across the street from my bedroom and people packed the streets while strolling hand-in-hand. Cafes provided a reprieve for those worn out by the constant walking to and from everywhere and a place where people gathered to connect. The French knew how to work hard and they understood the importance of play too. Time traveled slowly on the other side of the world. It was contrary to the fast-paced life in the United States where people worked fifty to sixty hours a week to achieve status and happiness. It seemed as if French people lived moment to moment, while enjoying the beauty all around them.

Exploring each corner of France in the first month ener-
gized me on so many levels. I absolutely loved sitting at the
cafes, as I sipped a café au lait and ate a mouth-watering
pain au chocolat. The chocolate, a richly decadent cocoa,
melted in your mouth at precisely the right moment. Every
morning, I walked to the corner boulangerie to purchase
my daily coffee and baguette, which I smothered with goat
cheese and a scrumptious sweet strawberry jam. Afterward, the program took us on daily trips to various regions
of France to study the language and culture of the country.

Nicole and I met on one of those excursions and became
friends. She traveled with the University of California
Davis with about twenty others in her group. We hung
out regularly, while tasting the Rhône Valley wines. Our
American way of life clearly did not equip us with the
rigors of French eating. The courses seemed endless and
within a month we busted out of the seams of our pants,
prompting us to explore French fashion rather quickly.

On a bright and sunny day, we took an excursion to Annecy, nicknamed the Pearl of the French Alps. It sits between Lake Annecy and the Semnoz mountain located in
the Southeastern region of France. Beautiful would hardly
describe this picturesque, quaint city looking like it came
straight from a Disney fairytale story. I half expected the

townspeople to break out in song. Think Beauty and the Beast. The city overflowed with joy; the sun shined down on us as swans swam in the lake adjacent to the streets. The buildings were of various colors, each with a balcony adorned with red and white velvety roses and purple flowers. Annecy ranks as one of the most beautiful cities I've visited in my life. Clearly, I walked through the second phase of the cycle of transformation, *Desire.* Everything was exciting, new, and the **Desire** to change was great.

Once the initial excitement died down, I attacked the daunting task of becoming fluent in French. The language and the speed at which French people speak made my brain spin like being on the Space Mountain roller coaster at Disneyland. We thought we were prepared to live there with the French classes we took at AC and the other programs. However, we quickly realized that to become fluent, we needed to practice every day and remove the fear of making mistakes. I spent a considerable amount of time daily in front of a mirror, with a pencil in my mouth, a language trick they taught us at the University to help with the closure of our throats. The "r" and the "u" sounds took consistent concentration and intentionality to perfect. The French were a proud culture and expected the Americans to sound flawless in their pronunciation of their language. In fact, if you failed to pronounce your words correctly, they made you stay an additional thirty minutes after class.

After the first month, we moved in with our families. Luckily, they placed me with an older couple and their cat, Mozart. The man taught English at the same university I attended, and the woman was an English teacher at a high school. They were kind and patient with me as I adjusted to life there. They provided a stable environment and a beautiful room with a view overlooking a park where I spent time observing families and old men playing Pétanque, the French version of Bocce ball.

The first two months in France were the hardest. I am amazed at how a young, bright-eyed, and broken woman like me had the strength to leave her support system behind, move abroad, immerse herself in a foreign culture, and start to live again. I hid the truth of my broken engagement, which had shattered my view of love and my self-esteem into a million tiny pieces. I spent many nights crying alone in my bed. The thoughts dominating my mind were, *why didn't I see what everyone else saw? Did I really look at life through rose-colored glasses? Was I not worthy of love?*

Despite being in one of the most beautiful countries in the world, I felt helpless and sad. It took every bit of strength and determination to wake up every day and go explore life around me. I called my family almost every day, I needed to hear my mom's voice for comfort. She advised me to take it one step at a time and to use France as a positive distraction. I took long walks on the streets of Lyon, observed life all around me, sat in cafes and people watched, made friends from neighboring countries on the University tours we took weekly and traveled to other countries. By focusing on the connections I made with my French family, friends, and my AC group, my attitude changed as a result. Giving myself grace along the way, I saw the light on the other side of the darkness and took it one day at a time.

A few weeks after I moved into their apartment, my French parents decided it would be nice for me to meet their grown daughters and their friends. Madame Bony took time to prepare a six-course meal to welcome me into their home. By the fourth course I was full, so when she made her way to give me the following course, I politely declined saying, "No merçi, je suis pleine." I could immediately see by the **Reactions** on their faces that I said something inappropriate. They were all trying hard to not laugh. I could feel my face getting hot and red. Monsieur Bony sensing my discomfort finally broke the silence to ask in English if I wanted to know what I had said.

"Yes," I replied.

He said, "You said you were pregnant like a cow would be. You meant to say you were full, right?"

My cheeks flushed as I held back tears of frustration in front of all their guests, "Yes." I managed to say through clenched teeth. Although I wanted to stay silent throughout the rest of the night, I pushed forward, past my **EGO Identity**, which threatened to stop my quest to become fluent in French.

The next day I spent my time observing the Lyonnaise. I witnessed how preoccupied they were in the metro station and picked up their common sayings, which I practiced in the mirror daily. The women wore scarves despite the heat and dressed formally with heels. Pretty soon, I wore scarves and heels everywhere.

We even had a bet going with the other American students from AC to see who could go the longest without shaving their legs or armpits. It's no secret the French don't shave, we found this out pretty quickly. I went four months without shaving and called it a success. We also found out they rarely wear deodorant, but I'm one of those to shower twice a day, kind of gals, so that was clearly out of the question for me. Since I live in Texas, you can understand why! I utterly refused to participate in the no deodorant bet. What I loved the most about living in France was the ability to walk to and from places. The only caveat, dog poop everywhere! I watched where I stepped; otherwise, I'd end up regretting it. My family owned a car but used it sparingly. With gasoline prices so high it was more economical and healthier to walk. Several of us would meet at Plaçe Bellecour, a plaza in the middle of the city, to walk to our classes at the university three miles from the apartment.

Despite their rich and delicious food and wonderful people, some of the American students missed home and would meet up at the McDonald's in the center of the city to take a break and speak our native language. Being away from home tested my resilience, especially with a broken heart.

Over the course of the months in France, I received correspondence from other mentors of Generación América, wondering when I would come back to school. They explained the program wasn't the same without "the heart" not being there. They also revealed Rick proposed to yet another woman within months of my departure. She, along with another mentor, created a smear campaign to get rid of me. It was devastating to read those hurtful letters. I felt betrayed by him and others who threatened to remove me from the Board of Directors of the program, which had been my idea. I had worked tirelessly to get it off the ground; it seemed so unfair.

I knew what I needed to do. The time arrived for me to step up for my needs instead of always putting everyone else first. My parents agreed I needed to stay abroad the whole year. I couldn't control what happened in the United States. I could control my focus on doing what I came to do in France, to become fluent in their language and culture. It felt like the momentum of all the inner work I put in to find myself in France paid off, because my confidence **Emerged** and I felt stronger and more connected to myself and God than ever before.

So, I decided to remain in the exchange program until June of the following year. Upon making my decision, I felt like a weight lifted from my shoulders and heart. God removed all perceived obstacles one-by-one from my path, making it very clear what I needed to do.

Aside from contending with bullies during my high school years, one of my strengths includes the ability to form connections with others which helped me immensely abroad. Mom often told me creating connections was my super power as a kid. While overcoming this painful time in my life, I made friends easily, which helped support me emotionally. I surrounded myself with amazing, energetic, and loving people. Being trilingual helped me make friends from all over the world. It thrilled us to find out our program offered three-day weekends often, which provided us with a chance to explore neighboring countries. This gave me the opportunity to travel by bus, metro, and train, and I became more independent and confident. I learned to trust my instincts and tap into the power inside of me. In total, I visited seven European countries while abroad.

All along our professors told us the day we dreamt in French became the day we were truly fluent. When the day arrived, it thrilled me because I completed my transformation. My adaptability skills grew stronger as the months went by, and I used them to fully immerse myself in their language and culture. I went from a not-so-fluent American student to a fluent French student who wore heels, scarves, and drank tea with cream in the afternoons. By the end of my stay, no one viewed me as an American, they accepted me as European. It took months of practice and months of pushing past the **EGO Identity** surfacing from time to time. I used this time in my life to remind myself of the power inside of me. Whenever an occasion arose for me to speak up, I took it, knowing it would help me create the **SOUL Identity** of the fluent student.

For years, I wanted to find a job to lead me back to Europe so I could live there permanently; however, God had a different plan for me all along. He used my choice to study abroad to equip me with the lesson of resilience. This lesson came in handy during the darkest periods of my life. It reminded me of the power inside of me and kept me on my intended path despite the setbacks along the way. Resilience helped me confront Rick and the Board of Directors who were intent on removing me from my program. I fought them back and remained there till I graduated AC.

Scripture for Journaling, Meditation, or Prayer

Jeremiah 29:11 *For I know the plans I have for you, declares the Lord, plans to prosper you and not to harm you.*

God had a plan for me, to prosper me and not to harm me. He placed a Desire in my heart to travel abroad to France after my broken engagement. Time

travel to a time when you couldn't see His plan but stayed resilient to it. What Turning Point(s) were you facing? How did you push past your mind to emerge into your new circumstances?

Chapter 5
I Will Persevere

At twenty-four I got married, despite the gnawing in my gut telling me not to. As I held onto my father's arm, a battle to run or marry Frank waged in my heart. *How could I cancel after my parents spent all this money on the wedding and we were surrounded by my family and friends in a Catholic Church?* My future with Frank waited for me at the end of the aisle, but was it a future I wanted?

I knew in my heart, he wasn't the man for me. He was twelve years older and set in his ways. During our six-month courtship, I saw many red flags. Out in public he was kind and affectionate, but behind closed doors, he showed how judgemental and harsh he could be. He pretended to like some people because it benefited him socially to do so, and later would openly criticize them. He had two sides to him, and I didn't know which one represented his authentic nature. He seemed to be in a rush to get married which I didn't quite understand then. He was thirty-six-years-old and likely felt the familial pressure to find a bride, marry and have a baby, almost like he was checking things off his to-do list.

Two weeks before my wedding, we broke up after a terrible fight. Mom's **Intuition** kicked into high gear and she firmly stated, "Sylvia, he's not the man for you!" I yelled back with tears in my eyes, "Yes, he is!" I acted on the feeling instead of allowing my logic to help me make the choice. This decision to marry a man I knew was not good for me came from my **Limiting Belief**, "I am ugly."

Deep down, I didn't think I would ever receive another marriage proposal. I didn't believe myself to be beautiful enough for anyone to ask again. This **Limiting Belief** stemmed from my years of being bullied in high school, were reinforced when I married him, and shows how I allowed these beliefs to steer my life choices.

Many people considered it the most beautiful ceremony they had ever seen. However, I didn't see the beauty in me. When I would look in a mirror, I would only see my imperfections. As a teenager, I developed severe acne. I used heavy makeup to cover the scars left by the pimples. I never saw or acknowledged my beautiful blue eyes or voluminous flowing brown hair. As far as I was concerned,

I was ugly. Years of bullying in high school did their job of crushing my confidence.

My chest felt tight as I gripped my father's arm, my legs shook underneath my two-piece heavy crepe dress, and the walls of the church closed in on me as we slowly made our way to the man I'd soon call husband.

My sense of doing the right thing kept me from calling it off despite God's voice telling me not to do it. As the oldest child, I felt in charge of setting the example for my siblings. *What kind of example would I give them by not following through on the commitment I'd made to Frank by saying yes to his proposal?* My heart and mind knew it would not work, but I didn't listen.

Pretending to be Happy

How can you live happily ever after when you start off on the wrong foot? Did I love him? Eventually I did, but I was not "in love" with him. I have no doubt he loved me in his way. However, I believed he chose me because I represented what he secretly craved, social acceptance and financial status. As well as, it helped to be young, and whom many considered to be beautiful, and I came from a good family. My job status and respectable income with the pharmaceutical giant Hoffman La Roche completed the package of all of his criteria. Our fast courtship led many to believe he loved what I did for him more than me.

During our honeymoon, he asked me what bills I would pay. In Hispanic culture, this question is considered taboo, since the man is supposed to provide for the wife and household. In fact, the Catholic tradition of exchanging gold coins during the wedding ceremony symbolizes this idea. What an odd question to ask on our honeymoon. At the moment, I wondered if he married me for his own goals of achieving financial success, and never completely trusted him after this. My dad's voice revealed his displeasure when I shared this situation with him, and said, "That's not something a man asks his wife on the honeymoon."

For years, my family and close friends suspected I wasn't happy. We carried this underlying tension between us, but I was determined to make it work. Around other people you would never know the deep pit of loneliness I lived in, while he put on his show of love. In church on Sundays, he would lovingly hold my hand while others looked on. At home he retreated to watch football. On the outside, I pretended we enjoyed a happy and loving relationship. His family believed we were an ideal match. Whereas, my family knew from the beginning we were not meant to be together. They couldn't understand my intention behind my **Actions**, and sadly I couldn't either. Many thought we lived a healthy and happy marriage.

At home he focused on his work, but rarely hugged or kissed me. It seemed now that he had me as his wife, the chase or excitement was over for him. When I suggested doing things together he would rarely say yes to it. In truth, we had very little in common. He didn't know how to show affection except out in public, when it felt like a show for all to see and accept him. In our private life he watched television, rarely held my hand, or kissed me, and would rather spend time drinking and making dinner with "the boys," his group of friends.

Work as an Escape

In 2001, just two years after we married, doctors diagnosed my dad with a benign brain tumor. Fear gripped me for the next two years, until the doctors explained he had to have surgery to remove it. However, I stayed focused on my work and I excelled at my job. By this point I moved from Roche to Pfizer Pharmaceuticals, the worldwide leader in pharmaceutical sales. I worked in their primary care division, selling major products to medical doctors in their offices. I won multiple awards, giving us a chance to travel to various parts of the country.

By March 2003, Dad, at the peak of his career as an Urologist, decided to remove the benign tumor. The doctors at the Mayo Clinic explained if it continued growing, he would simply not wake up one day. Dad cared deeply about his family and his patients, and wanted to do the best for everyone involved. He scheduled his surgery with a surgeon in Arkansas who was highly specialized in his type of tumor.

Work became my escape from the fear and great pain at the thought of losing him. I couldn't control my dad's tumor or the possibility of him dying on the surgery table, but working long hours gave my energy and fear something useful to do. This **Turning Point** and shift in my life created another pattern, and shows up during times of enormous stress.

Although Daddy survived twenty-four hours of surgery, he suffered an ischemic stroke after the second surgery the following day, which left him paralyzed on his left side. He slowly regained his strength, but he never fully recovered.

I spent all of my vacation days in Arkansas with my family, supporting my mom. The outcome clearly devastated her. She excused herself periodically to walk out of his room to sob uncontrollably. She paced aimlessly in the hospital corridors with a blank look on her face. My sister or I would stay behind, holding his hand as his team of doctors performed painful procedures to relieve the swelling in his neck. Dad, my hero, toughed it out in front of us, to protect us while he smiled weakly. His eyes winced as they stuck a long needle into his neck to relieve the pressure. Clenching my fists, I held back the tears threatening to disrupt the peace in the room.

I'd steal a glance at my baby sister, who attempted to do the same. We took turns with Dad to give each other the space to grieve alone. Each of us attempted to be strong for the other one.

A week after his procedure, I walked into his room and witnessed two physical therapists lifting his limp body from his wheelchair to help him regain his gait. Witnessing my once-strong Dad during the therapy sessions was difficult and painful to watch. He'd become so weak and dependent on others for basic needs. Daddy had already survived so much in his life, it just seemed so unfair. *What happened to the indestructible, powerful, and confident dad who pushed us to succeed? Would he ever go back to being the same man? What was Mom going to do? How would this change their relationship?*

A Professional Life Cut Short

Despite recovering enough to return to work on a limited basis, the tumor cut his career short. His colleagues left him one-by-one, which broke my heart to watch. I worked with him for years in his office during my summers in high school and as a representative with Pfizer selling products to him. Since I worked in the healthcare environment, I observed how slowly and cruelly everyone he worked with left him. They believed the rumors flying around while he recovered in rehab. Two of his partners visited him and came back to spread malicious rumors about the stroke incapacitating his mental capabilities and said he hovered near the brink of death.

As I rounded in several hospital units, I overheard people whispering, "Did you hear, Villalobos is near death? No, I didn't know. Really? I guess we should refer all our patients to the urologist in the next town over."

Daddy served as an integral part of the medical community on numerous boards of directors, at times leading them as Chairman of the Board. As his daughter, it hurt to watch how his "friends" refused to support him except for one, Dr. Victor Gonzalez. He continued to refer patients to him. His colleagues shut off every possibility for him to regain a sense of purpose. These were the same individuals my daddy helped immensely during his career, and now when he needed them, they abandoned him. This devastated his practice and despite coming back to work on a limited basis, Daddy retired from medicine four years later in 2007.

Mom became his primary caregiver. She devoted her life to ensuring he got back on his feet. Empowering him daily with strenuous hand exercises to strengthen his left side became a common theme at home. By appealing to his competitive nature, he quickly rebounded from the stroke. The tender way in which she helped bathe, shave, and dress him contributed to their blossoming love affair. Mom often said, "It's my privilege to serve him. He's the wind beneath my wings." This **Turning Point** in their marriage shifted their focus. Since Dad's friends essentially abandoned him, Mom once again became his one loyal friend. They ate meals together and watched countless shows, often talking throughout.

The years following his stroke helped Mom and Dad become closer than ever and it was beautiful to watch. What came out of so much pain renewed our closeness as a family. We all used our strengths to help during this time. Both my brother and sister helped with the medical aspects, while I helped with keeping their bills paid on time, and taking care of their home while out of state for medical appointments. Daddy learned over time the family he created made up the most important part of his life. Although he'd grown up without a strong family foundation, a **Turning Point** like this one made him realize that he'd created the loving support he'd always wanted.

Love on the Rocks

Escaping into my work and helping my parents kept me away from my home. Anyone close to me at the time could sense I avoided spending time with my husband. I felt a purpose, and it drove me to do more. But in retrospect, this revealed the **Avoider** pattern in my life. The pain of witnessing my dad lose his practice only drove me into a frenzy of activity to avoid the realization my home life lacked the love and connection I craved.

My first marriage lived on the rocks for years and my fear kept me from facing the reality of my choices. I didn't feel a strong connection with him. It felt more like a roommate situation. Yet I continued to feed the facade that we lived the perfect life. As a high **Achiever** and **Perfectionist**, I felt I could not fail. The "what ifs" kept me from leaving. Clearly, I lived in my fearful **EGO Identity** for many years.

Everyone around me felt my unhappiness and saw it on my face and in my actions. Some friends and family tried to talk to me about it, but I *pretended* my marriage filled me with happiness and meaning. I mastered the art of pretending and as a coach now I see how the habit formed.

My husband asked to have a child for many years, but I held off. It gave me some aspect of control over my life. After my father almost died, I decided to finally have a child. I wanted my parents to experience being grandparents, and I feared they would die before they received the chance. My father's illness triggered my fear into **Action**.

The Joys of Motherhood

In May 2005, we welcomed our son Andres into the world. I can honestly say looking into his dark eyes, touching his soft skin, and listening to his little baby cries made it the happiest day of my life. I loved becoming a mom. Pfizer gave several weeks off for maternity leave, which I gladly took. Those first few days, despite my C-section, were magical. I couldn't contain the love for this little boy. He quickly became my whole world. I instinctively knew how to hold, change and feed him. During the night when he cried for a feeding, my body jumped out of bed, regardless of the physical pain I felt in my mid-section. I spent the night gazing at him with wonderment. *How could I love someone this completely? How did I get so lucky to have such a beautiful baby boy? Thank you, God, for this gift of love you sent me.* The love I felt for him filled my heart and **SOUL**.

Motherhood suited me well, however, I felt a pull to return to work. I conditioned myself to rely on work to express my value as a woman in this world, and a big part of me itched to get back on the saddle again.

Losing the Slam Dunk

Halfway into my leave, my boss called to inform me a specialty representative position would open soon. He knew of my **Desire** for a promotion. I talked with Frank and we decided for me to end maternity leave early to apply for the position. Despite loving this stage, my goal, and dream for years, had included promoting up in the company. I believed women could have it all, career and life balance.

Many at Pfizer considered me the best candidate for the position because of the number of sales awards, work ethic, and tenure. Our manager and the representative, another man to be our partner, conducted the interviews. I always interviewed well and served as an integral part of their team helping our manager, Dan, conduct interviews. I knew the process well and prepared for it. What I failed to understand was the denial of the promotion, because I did not have enough speaker programs. These were dinners held with doctors, where a speaker spoke on the product. I didn't have a sufficient number of these on the books for the year despite my many years of having them. The guy who received the position had only been with the company for six months, but was well-liked by the other specialty representative. The rumor running around said he did not like me, and his vote mattered in the process.

I remember the day my manager called to give me the news. Early on I knew they did not pick me and remember feeling betrayed and humiliated. The rest of the team was clearly outraged over their choice. How could they give it to someone who had not proven himself at the job?

What's Next?

As soon as we hung up, Mom called to ask me about it. The tears flowing, make-up ruined, and voice barely a whisper, I managed to explain between sobs. She suggested we take the day off and walk on the beach. Mom arrived within fifteen minutes and we drove to South Padre Island to spend quality time together. I put on the baby carrier and carried Andres up and down the beach all day.

I contemplated leaving the company. Another district manager from Houston who left Pfizer, heard the news and called me directly the same day to offer me a higher position. There were so many decisions swirling around in my head and the noise became too loud. In times like these, it's best to quiet the mind and detach from the emotion. I detached from my feelings of betrayal and humiliation to make the logical decision for my life. I also asked God for guidance, for He knew my path in life. A voice inside of me said, "Stay." I interrupted my anger and decided to trust the voice inside of me.

God said, "Stay."

I stayed at the company and worked hard for a promotion. I believed in my ability and held onto my belief that one day I would be promoted. This shift also solidified my perseverance to achieve goals. In the next two years, they denied promotions for me two more times, but every time I learned something new; I could improve on when the next opportunity presented itself. Every time another male colleague received the promotion, and they told me no, it only strengthened my belief God would deliver when the time was right.

My perseverance paid off, because in May 2007, I received the promotion to the Hospital Division at Pfizer Pharmaceuticals. This position they considered higher than the specialty positions I interviewed for numerous times. Interestingly enough, when the layoffs started at Pfizer, they spared my position whereas all the other positions denied to me were laid off.

God is for you!

One of the most important lessons I've learned that helps me get through challenging times is understanding that everything happens *for* you and not *to* you! With God in your corner, it will happen on His timing, not yours. He knows what's best for you and where you will shine!

My confidence obtained a significant boost with my promotion. I felt as though the beliefs I held for myself paid off. However, I lived in survival mode in my professional and personal life. I inherited the worst territory in my sales region. It rated second to last in sales, meaning I had little time to prove myself. The rumor mill believed I didn't have what it took to turn the territory around and was not the best candidate.

As a child of Mexican immigrants, my family and parents instilled in me the work ethic to be successful at a young age. My identity and happiness were tied to proving my worth through achievements. I had believed that when I arrived at this mythical pinnacle of success, meaning the highest achievement at Pfizer and the number one spot in sales, happiness would follow. I fixated on my goals to prove my worth to the company and to myself, because deep down, *"I didn't feel worthy enough."*

Circumstances continued to reinforce this belief as a child and throughout my life. I longed for the attention of others, especially my father's. With every achievement, I would ask him if he was proud of me. Instead, he would use the opportunity to share how I could've been a lawyer or gotten my master's degree, two things he attached to being successful. My dad spent every waking hour working to provide us with a better life. Our one-week vacation a year with him represented the only quality time he spent with us. He left our home at 6:30 am and returned late in the evening. My **Subconscious Mind** associated his work with abandonment, the thinking that "I am not enough for my dad." To prove my worth in this company, I created a habit around working fifty to sixty hours a week, something my father modeled to me.

I Must Achieve To Feel Enough!

The one thing I didn't like about my dad, I now formed the same habit and modeled it to my young son. Today I understand the power of my **Subconscious Mind**. It relied on the programming I gave it and operated on automatic, meaning, I did not deliberately know what I did or how it steered my choices in life. The **Achiever** reared its ugly head to repeat my dad's programming to my own boy. As an **Achiever**, I put my head down and worked hard anytime I hit an obstacle in my personal or professional life. I was focused on the end goal which was to be happy and believed wholeheartedly that my successes would bring fulfillment. I craved the significance this achievement would likely give me and the attention I would receive from my bosses. I strove to succeed to the point of exhaustion, because deep down I didn't feel worthy and longed to gain the acceptance of others, especially my Father's.

The battle ensues between the EGO and the SOUL

Change came roaring at me and with it came a battle between my **EGO** and **SOUL**. These two identities showed up to fight it out with the tension in my marriage, Dad's stroke and my promotion. On the one hand, my mind where my **EGO** resided fed me the **Limiting Beliefs** and patterns of "I'm not enough" and "I must achieve;" while

God placed a **Desire** in my heart to be number one in the sales territory and that led to my promotion. God heard my prayers and knew what was coming down my path. He used change as an opportunity to showcase my perseverance. I felt a pull to step into it with excitement, but my mind tested my resolve every step of the way. Doubtful thoughts like, *it's impossible to turn it around* and *you don't have what it takes to make this happen* began to pester me daily. There were those who reinforced these thoughts while others like my mom and close partners empowered me to step into it with my tenacity and passion, spiritual gifts God gave me. When I interrupted the noise inside my head and replaced it with visions of standing on stage in front of my peers at our annual regional awards dinner, I felt compelled to work towards this **Desire**.

I strategically outlined the greatest opportunities to gain momentum in my sales. I focused on what I could do instead of what I was restricted from doing. I began to call on the smaller accounts and on those I had established relationships with throughout the years.

Hospital rules made it practically impossible to walk in and speak to those responsible for using the type of medication I promoted. Most of the patients that benefited from them were found in Intensive Critical Units, (ICU), which meant I would need to find a way to get in front of doctors who prescribed them and they worked exclusively in the hospital.

Mark, my boss, taught us to walk into the hospitals without appointments and make as many contacts as possible so we could get into them easier. This tactic came with dire consequences if caught by the Director of Pharmacy who oversaw the representatives in the hospitals. I could be permanently barred from entering.

The day arrived when I walked into the hospital without an appointment. My legs shook uncontrollably under my pants but I held onto the belief and vision that I would walk on stage to receive the number one position in my territory. I took a deep breath and made my way confidently to the floors. I carried an air of belonging with me as I got into the elevator, and a little notebook where I planned to take down the names of the directors of each floor. Mark gave our team the goal to speak to at least three people on each floor. I felt relieved three hours later when I emerged with pages of contacts and vital information! I could feel God doing a victory dance in Heaven and saying, "That's my girl!"

In faith, I thrive

Several years after abandoning the Catholic Church, my **SOUL** felt a pull to seek God with all my heart. A need developed to establish an intimate relationship with Him. The feeling inside of me was to allow God to guide me through major change by trusting His voice instead of my mental **EGO** jargon. I began talking to Him through my thoughts and then through my writing. In my daily early morning journaling sessions, God's love and strength came through. I felt his presence and encouragement to continue knocking on doors despite the many No's I encountered. Journaling helped quiet the mean and demeaning thoughts of disbelief that sometimes wanted to question my ability to be number one. In my faith, with God by my side, I began to thrive.

Within four months of my placement, I got my first prescription of the product that had never been sold. I beat my regional bosses' prediction that it would take six months before seeing any sales. This little momentum gave me the boost I needed to push past any remaining doubts that I was not the right person for the job. It only took the first person and before I knew it, several accounts ordered the product to be stocked in their hospitals. Within six months, my territory began to creep up and by the end of 2007, seven months later, I ranked in the top ten of my

region and country. This trend would continue throughout 2008. I achieved what most deemed impossible but I
knew with God in my corner, everything and anything was
possible!

Scripture for Journaling, Meditation, or Prayer

James 1:12 *Blessed is the one who perseveres under trial
because, having stood the test, that person will receive the
crown of life that the Lord has promised to those who love
Him.*

**When in your life did you persevere in circumstances
that threatened to thwart your security? How did it
test you? What lessons did you learn about yourself?**

Chapter 6
I Will Be Faithful

On July 23, 2008, Frank and I sat in awkward silence while our four-year-old quietly played in the next room, and Hurricane Dolly stormed over our South Texas home. I could barely hear the creak of Frank rocking in the chair we used to rock our son as a baby over the wind. The power went out, and the wind roared outside. It ripped the roof to shreds, sending pieces flying to the front of our home as water dripped from the opening in the living room ceiling onto the hardwood floor. It made it hard to focus and hear him.

He asked, "How long have we been in therapy?"

I answered, "Seven months."

In a very matter-of-fact voice, he dropped a bomb on me, "I think we should get a divorce."

For a moment, I believed I heard wrong. "What did you say? We should get a divorce?" My fight-or-flight mechanism kicked into gear. "You want to leave us? What about Andres? Have you thought about what this will do to him? Please, don't do this to our family."

He continued rocking calmly with a blank stare on his face and with determination in his voice said, "What's there to think about?"

All the blood drained from my face, and I could hardly breathe. Somewhere deep inside, a wave of relief washed through me. It took a moment for me to fully understand the impact of his words. I begged him to reconsider, to think of our little boy, and what this would do to him. I asked him to think about it until Saturday, which gave him three days. He reluctantly agreed to hold off until then.

I woke up on Saturday morning with a feeling of dread in the pit of my stomach. *I wonder what he decided. Would he stick to his decision to end our marriage?* I attempted to read his face all day as I quietly dressed in a bright pink outfit, hoping to make my crystal blue eyes stand out and to show off my hour-glass figure. Sheepishly, I asked him how I looked.

He barely glanced up and responded rather coolly, "Fine."

En route to dinner, I hesitantly broached the subject once more, my fear of the unknown slowly creeping up. He adamantly stuck to his initial suggestion, divorce.

My marriage slowly unraveled, layer by layer, piece by piece until it disappeared. Every cell in my body knew, and yet when he asked for a divorce, it hit me like a ton of bricks. My chest tightened, and my breath hollowed. Fear of the unknown clenched my throat. *God, please give me the strength to pull through for my little boy. Stay and guide me, I don't know who to be or what to do.* I prayed for courage and faith. When Frank asked for the divorce in July 2008, I felt all the emotions of a loss, the pain of failure, and yet deep down I felt relieved and released.

We met our friend, Jaime, for dinner, but his wife, Julia, was out of town so it was just the three of us. The guys spent the next couple of hours drinking, eating, and laughing, while I stepped out countless times to the restroom and outside to cry. At one point, Frank called me on the phone to tell me to come back inside to eat, insisting I had a responsibility to our friend.

He spent the evening having the time of his life. I could not comprehend how a man who once vowed to love and protect me could be so callous. He decided to end our life together just hours earlier but hardly seemed fazed.

Persevering Through the Ups & Downs

We persevered through some major ups and downs in the nearly ten years we were together. Even though Frank and I started off on the wrong foot in our marriage, we made a strong team on the big events in our life. We supported each other in our dreams for promotion.

In the early years, I empowered him to branch off on his own and build his engineering and surveying business. Frank was a dedicated and hard worker who often got passed up for promotion. We agreed that my work in pharmaceuticals would serve as our income until he could build it to contribute to our finances. He boasted often with family and friends about how I supported his dream of owning his own business and how grateful he was to me. Likewise; when I expressed my **Desire** to be promoted, he took care of our son during the weekends so I could devote time to the preparation of the interviews.

We saw eye-to-eye on the importance of enjoying time with our family. We both were fond of spending weekends at my parents' beach house. I remember the four of us swimming in the ocean and afterwards eating a scrumptious dinner at a nice restaurant on the bay. When Dad announced his intention to have surgery, Frank scheduled time to spend it with us in Arkansas. He stayed a week after the surgery, chauffeuring us back and forth from the hotel to the hospital and taking family to and from the airport. My parents needed me to take care of their finances while they remained in rehab after his stroke. Frank, supported my need to be there for my family since it was his top value too.

As any long marriage can attest, there are good and bad times in it. Unfortunately for us, there were more downs than ups. My marriage taught me that there was staying power when your values align, and ours did for a while. However, over time, I began to feel the significant age gap between us. While I was the more social one, Frank preferred staying and entertaining at home. I was athletic and heavily involved with tennis leagues while he wasn't athletic at all. The responsibilities at work stretched my capacity as a professional woman, and it began to change me for the better but that also changed the dynamic between us. Frank loved the benefits of my high pay but also wanted me to solely take care of our son and the home. This did not align to who I felt God was leading me to become. The opportunities He provided me with the promotion were in direct contradiction to the woman Frank wanted me to be.

The last big difference was the way we each viewed God and faith. Frank was one of the "hypocritical" people I encountered and whose **Actions** influenced the way I experienced God and religion. In church, Frank was attentive and affectionate with me and at home was distant and detached emotionally. During our ten year marriage, I lost my relationship with God and felt a significant void in my heart as a result. I **Desired** a union where God took center stage.

With my promotion came a newfound belief in my capacity to stretch completely out of my comfort zone. I know God placed this opportunity in my path to prepare me for the hardships ahead. My perseverance at home and at work taught me that I embodied the confidence to step in uncertainty with faith and belief.

It took this **Turning Point** in my life to shift me in the true direction of my life. I stopped being afraid, and I acted despite the uncertainty. God used this opportunity to interrupt my self-sabotaging, **Security Seeker** pattern once again. He showed my capacity to navigate change by trusting Him. This provided me with confidence, clarity, and courage for the events which would rock my certainty again in the coming years.

God certainly equipped me for the unknown future and many more challenging situations down the road. I trusted His voice in me as I navigated the waters, and I felt less alone in my journey. I thank God for these ten years, for they gave me such joy, exquisite pain, and lessons learned I am applying today.

What If?

The next couple of days were a blur. *How could I break the news to our little boy? Would I survive on my own?* The biggest "what if" which kept me from following my **God Instinct** to leave before he asked for the divorce. *Would I be able to make enough to support my little boy and the two women that I vowed to help?* Guadalupe and Rosy worked tireless hours as nannies and housekeepers on weeks I needed to travel for work. We hired Guadalupe when I was still pregnant with Andres, and Rosy joined two years later on days Guadalupe could not work. They provided for their own families as the sole breadwinners. Guadalupe, a widow, and mom to four children had the greatest faith and relationship with God I'd seen despite the loss of her husband and child two years apart. Rosy's husband could not work due to an injury so she worked in several homes to make enough to support her family. Both of these women witnessed the disintegration of our marriage and were often there when I would break down and cry, sometimes offering a bit of advice or a comforting shoulder. I was determined to keep them employed. I secretly vowed to God I would help them regardless of the outcome.

The integration between work and my home life as a single mom proved harder than I imagined. What is the right amount of work and play in life? My modeling from my childhood distorted my view of balance. I became the provider overnight, and yet I held myself to the unattainable standard of motherhood I'd learned from my mom. My mom was a stay-at-home-parent who participated 100% in my activities, who volunteered at booster clubs, took me to all events, made me home cooked meals, and was my emotional cheerleader.

I felt torn between providing for my son's needs financially and being there as my mom was there for me. I wanted to be an involved parent with Andres, and I wanted to make enough to keep my son in his private school and the only home he'd ever known. These were two recommendations our therapist made to us.

I navigated uncharted waters. My family did not know how to help me. My parents could not relate to the inner dilemma I suffered because divorce wasn't a common occurrence in our large extended Mexican family. Mom thought telling me to be home more would help the situation. She couldn't relate to my feelings of responsibility since she enjoyed life at home with her kids without the pressure of providing. Dad was the provider and he ensured Mom did not have to work so she could be there with us. Randy, my therapist, told us from the beginning of the separation, "Andres needs stability. The less you change his environment, the better his adjustment." My mind kept replaying this conversation. It fed the need to achieve more money to keep us in the house we lived in; with an astounding mortgage for a town like Brownsville, Texas. It also fed the need to keep Andres in the private school he attended. When I asked Frank to help me with his school he bluntly said, "I'll give you what is required of me but nothing more." Clearly, his idea of following an expert's advice differed significantly from mine.

Rely on God and See Your Life Transform

There were so many unanswered questions inside of me. Unfortunately, my fear was a strong motivator that kept me stuck in the what ifs. Since the age of seven, my layers of doubt taught me to rely on my understanding instead of releasing the "how" to my Heavenly Father. During the early days of the separation, I felt a pull to fully rely on Him, and surrender all my worries to Him, a concept that up until this **Turning Point**, was completely foreign to me. The high emotions depleted my energy and I needed help from Him. Daily, I relied on prayer to guide me through those initial days of disbelief and awakening. I prayed to God to give me the emotional support and strength to put one foot in front of the other. Having a small son who depended on me actually saved me. My immense love for him allowed me to put pride, hate, and resentment aside to focus on my beautiful, innocent child.

The days leading up to Frank picking up his things and furniture from the home we once shared were the hardest to live through. During this time, I formed a closer connection to God, and my spiritual transformation truly began. As a child, I believed in God and was taught to pray, yet I didn't truly understand or practice a relationship with Him. I quieted my mind and journaled once again to connect to the mind of God daily—not just in moments of distress. The practice of releasing my resentment and pain to him became a habitual practice, helping me navigate my journey after the separation.

Would I have the strength to face Frank? By praying to God and releasing those feelings, I left it in God's hands. When the day finally arrived, peace and calm covered me the entire day! It was a deeply impactful experience that shifted my relationship with God and showed me I could fully rely and have faith in Him.

As a Spiritual Transformation Coach, I see the shifts and the patterns interrupted by the divorce as I write these words. The **Perfectionist Pattern of Behavior** significantly contributed to prolonging my stay in the empty marriage. I pretended my life fulfilled me because deep down I didn't believe to be worthy enough on my own. On the outside I looked like I had it all together, but my **Limiting Beliefs** were the true drivers of my actions during our marriage. The divorce came to interrupt this pattern in my life and lift the veil from my eyes. It also came to halt my *Security Seeker* pattern. I stayed comfortable in my misery for too long and needed to move on. Despite feeling fear, I stepped into it with determination, courage, and undying faith. I had a four-year-old son to live for and think about.

My EGO Identity Takes Center Stage

My work at Pfizer Pharmaceuticals served as a tremendous blessing because it allowed me the choice to walk away with financial stability from the marriage that was suffocating me in more ways than one. God provided me with this job as a source of financial comfort, for He knew my path and the intentions of others. The financial responsibility I felt to keep my child in his home and school and Guadalupe and Rosy employed drove my need to work more than I needed to. My **EGO Identity**, as a **Perfectionist** and high achiever, launched me into overdrive, while my fear of failure motivated me to work long hours every week. The delicate balance between my employment and personal life became my biggest challenge as a single parent.

My son needed me to be there to help him navigate this time. However, my pesky **Avoider** pattern showed up and I stopped my therapy sessions during the first year of my divorce. I felt depleted emotionally and physically dealing with the role I played in the dissolution of my marriage and looked for escape through my work and in projects at home. The hurricane, whose eye circled the Rio Grande Valley, wrecked the house and I ended up with flood damage to the exterior and interior parts of my home. I escaped into the many projects to keep up with the repairs, avoiding my pain at all costs.

My little boy would often ask me, "Mom, do you really need to go back to work?" I'd get down to his level, hug him as I answered yes, and promptly leave. The memory of the sadness reflected on his face as my car pulled away from the house to make one last call of the day haunted me for many years afterwards. The truth was, I didn't really have to, yet my feeling of failure pulled me to leave the place that most reminded me of my personal defeat, my home. In my mind, I ultimately failed my son, the only innocent party to this, because I couldn't make our marriage work. This fear sabotaged any joy or blessing God tried to give me and instead I placed all the blame on me as moms often do. It's called "mom guilt," and it has tremendous potential to ruin your relationships with yourself and most importantly with your kids. **Awareness** today helps me understand that staying in therapy, taking ownership for my role in the dissolution of my marriage, and releasing my feelings of guilt to God, would be the healthiest way to address this internal dilemma that blocked me from moving forward in joy.

My **Subconscious Mind** used the internal dialogue of, *I don't have the bandwidth to deal with my pain right now* to keep me focused on something other than the situation at home with my boy. Throughout my divorce I made many mistakes, but this was my biggest mistake. By avoiding my pain, I prolonged my emotional, spiritual and physical healing and that of my son's.

Our divorce created a significant emotional event affecting Andres' belief systems. His little four-year-old heart felt abandoned by his father and confused why Daddy couldn't live with us anymore. He likely developed an "I am not enough" **Limiting Belief** as a result of this significant emotional event. His cry for his dad broke my heart on the many nights I held my sweet boy and reassured him of the love from his dad. By not getting help myself, I did not know properly how to help my son navigate his pain and, in the end, modeled what my dad modeled to me without being aware of my **Actions**. Mental and emotional health are important aspects to take care of during major transitions like divorce.

In retrospect now, I realize because of my stress during this time, patterns showed up in part to protect me (the **Subconscious Mind's** job) and in a bigger part to keep me from working through the **EGO Identity** showing up in my life.

My Promotion Was a Blessing from God

My company promoted me to my dream job. As the months rolled by, my **Desire** to be number one grew stronger everyday. I used the bad energy from my former spouse's rejection as motivation to believe in myself and my capacity as a corporate professional and as a loving mom. During my teenage years, when bullying was at its height, Mom taught me to use the energy of a bad situation for good. It was her way of getting me to see the light in a dark place. I used this tactic to motivate me to be God's child and shine His light. He was giving me the opportunity with this **Turning Point** to learn the lesson of faith in Him. When I accepted the promotion at Pfizer Pharmaceuticals, I assumed control of an underperforming territory. My boss, Mark, trusted me to take over a position previously occupied by someone who failed to sell the products that would ultimately save lives and left it in terrible shape. He discussed at length with me the pressure I would be under by his bosses to turn the territory around because it dragged the sales numbers down for the region. The senior vice-president also voiced his concerns. They pressured me immensely to perform at very high levels.

When I took over the territory, there were many who didn't believe I could turn it around, including many on the leadership team. I waited four years for this promotion and I finally made it into this role. The sales territory stood in shambles, but I believed in my ability to boost sales. I possessed the passion, patience, and perseverance to do it.

Because I slid into my **Avoider** pattern and allowed fear to dictate my actions, I became an **Achiever**. I created **Habits** around my patterns and by default I tied my identity to being successful at work. Balancing my career and home life became a challenge.

These patterns need to be identified and interrupted, otherwise you'll end up like me, regretting your mistakes and carrying around shame and guilt which can keep you stuck.

Change is An Opportunity God Gives You!

My **Limiting Beliefs** drove my **Action** to work harder than needed. In my Mexican culture, there is a belief that gets passed down, one generation to the next, which is that a woman can't have everything unless she sacrifices something. It became my own belief the more I thought about it. The self-sabotaging habit of working long hours to avoid my pain affected my personal time at home. I required therapy to face my responsibility in my failed marriage, identify my patterns of behavior, and deal with the lingering emotions from the divorce. In those years, my relationship with God was in the infancy stages, because my fear steered more of my choices instead of God's promptings. I believed in Him and began to speak to Him more and more everyday, but I needed to trust Him, a concept difficult for someone used to being in control of her life, only then could I truly be there for my son. The confusion I felt about my role in my son's life impacted him. That impact devastated him, even though I never intended to hurt or ignore him. After realizing my mistake in behavior, ten years later, I apologized to my fourteen-year-old son. He admitted he felt abandoned by both his parents during this time.

I wasn't consciously aware of my actions during this time in my life, which meant that my **Subconscious Mind**, the feeling mind, was truly in control of me. It bridged the gap in my **Awareness** with the programming I fed it daily, through my thoughts, attitudes and belief. It then reacted on automatic pilot.

The divorce was the opportunity God used to interrupt my **Security Seeker** and **Perfectionist** patterns, which had kept me in a loveless marriage for too long. He provided me the chance to rid myself of these layers of trauma I carried around as my armor of protection. I faced uncertainty with the courage, belief, and responsibility from the strength that turning to God during times of change gave me. It helped me direct the energy into my work, which provided for me and for the others under my responsibility.

Patterns rarely show up or surface, rather, they work incognito, meaning you are completely unaware of them. Divorce created uncertainty and forced me to step out of my comfort zone. For years, I endured an unhappy life. I found the power within me, by relying on God and for the first time in ten years I depended solely on me. It elevated my belief in myself and I soared. In the year of immense pain, I turned an underperforming territory standing dead last in my region of 364 representatives to number one and number two in the country in sales. I did the impossible, despite the many naysayers who didn't believe in my abilities to do the job.

I Did the *Best* Job I Consciously Knew How

Before the divorce, I operated from Fear, afraid to step out on my own. This massive change in status became a blessing in disguise. It guided me to get closer to God and challenged me to become the empowered woman God created me to be. With His guidance I transformed my life in a beautiful way.

Among the many lessons I learned from my divorce, there were two in particular that stood out. I needed to stay faithful to God's timing and get help uncovering my **Limiting Beliefs**.

I did the best job I consciously knew how at the time. Despite the countless hours I dedicated at work to turn it into a winning territory, I showed up for all the important moments in my son's life. There is always room for improvement and I know now I could have done a better job of being there more for my little boy. What became instrumental in my healing was forgiving myself and releasing to God the feelings of shame and guilt I carried around for ten years. It's evident to me now that the key to success is seeking help from a coach or therapist while going through **Turning Points** to have an objective observer in your life.

If I could turn back time I would seek balance first. Channeling my pain into something productive served me well in my teenage years to survive bullying, but it sabotaged my joy and reinforced these patterns in me as a single adult. If I had taken an inventory of my belief systems and focus, I likely would have seen the imbalance sooner.

My goal in sharing these painful memories of my divorce with you is my act of love for all the single parents living this experience right now. I want you to know I understand your need to feel significant and to feel the value you bring through your work. I've been there. The rejection triggered me and the feeling of unworthiness drove my **Actions**. The only thing I felt in control of was my work, which filled the void of unworthiness I felt inside. I avoided the pain by working.

I found God during one of the darkest periods of my life. Relying on Him, His promptings, and His guidance helped me find the way out of the darkness. I formed a strong connection with Him, and by default, with myself. My strength and belief in my capacity grew exponentially. It showed me my strength, my courage, my adaptability, and my belief in myself. I was there to support others instrumental in my success as a mother and as a corporate professional. By channeling my pain into my work, I accomplished a goal that set me up financially for the divorce. My light shined brightly by believing in myself and my capacity. I learned to create happiness, and I found the character and integrity living inside of me.

Scripture for Journaling, Meditation or Prayer

Psalm 37: 3-7 *Trust in the Lord and do good; dwell in the land and enjoy safe pasture. Take delight in the Lord and He will give you the desires of your heart. Commit your way to the Lord; trust in Him and He will do this; He will make your righteous reward shine like the dawn, your vindication like the noonday sun. Be still before the Lord and wait patiently for Him; do not fret when people succeed in their ways, when they carry out their wicked schemes.*

Sometimes in life we encounter situations that make us doubt doing the right things because we experience others doing selfish things to get ahead, like I did with Frank during the divorce. As the scripture above states, wait patiently for God, do not fret when people succeed in their ways.... Think of a time when you did the right thing even when it was hard to do so. How did that experience transform your view of yourself, and others?

Chapter 7
I Am a Visionary

I went back to therapy a year after my divorce and spent the next year and half in therapy. I rolled up my sleeves and put in the time to heal my emotional wounds because I wanted to date again. It felt silly when Randy, my therapist, asked me to visualize how it would feel when I met "the one." We developed a list of physical and emotional qualities of my soulmate. Next, I visualized how the meeting would happen, then my mind would "know" based on the information I gave my brain.

This is awkward. I feel weird doing this. Okay, close my eyes, sit on a chair in a theater and watch myself on screen with my soulmate? Did I get that right? What am I supposed to do now? Oh, yes, I remember, feel how the interaction would go.

I opened my eyes and Randy asked, "How did the meeting feel?" When he saw the blank look on my face, he said. "It takes practice, Sylvia. Your power is inside of you, use it."

Five minutes daily is all it took to put the force of my imagination to work in my favor. I'd sit quietly in the mornings with my steaming cup of coffee, put on instrumental music, close my eyes and imagine. He was blonde, blue eyes, built, affectionate, accepting of my son, and loving. I placed my hands on my heart and envisioned our curiosity as we discovered each other. The more I did it, the more I felt the shift inside of me. It took consistency, intentionality, and focus daily to condition my mind to the emotions. I looked forward to my sessions with Randy as I mastered this technique.

Dating in the Valley proved disastrous. Men were solely interested in sleeping with me and intimidated by my job and home. Profiles on eHarmony and Match became my first attempts at dating outside of my comfort zone. I widened the area into San Antonio, Austin, and Houston. Interestingly, the dating sites encouraged men to post pictures with their kids, yet when women did, they rarely received any hits. I received zero clicks when I posted with my son, and more clicks and winks if I posted a sexy picture of me. Double standard at its finest! Quickly, I realized Randy's advice to travel outside of the city would be my best bet at finding *the one,* "Sylvia, pick up a new hobby and expand outside of your sphere of influence."

After the long journey of healing, my heart and mind were ready to settle down and build a home with my soulmate and son. The weekly sessions with my therapist helped me work with my **Subconscious Mind** by providing a mental picture of the attributes and feelings associated with the encounter.

Create the Vision of Your Life!

I was first introduced to creating a vision board at a women's gathering in 2007 and loved the concept of it. The leader of the workshop encouraged me to create a vision using images that appealed to me. She explained that the purpose of the vision board was to provide your mind with a picture of what you **Desired**.

Equipped with a pair of scissors and plenty of magazines, I began to shape my ideal life. I organized my poster board into the four most important pillars of my life: career, health, mindset and relationships. The board hung in my office for several years providing my **Subconscious Mind** with new feelings, thoughts, beliefs, attitudes, self-talk and **SOUL Habits** that aligned to the vision.

In 2011, after a therapy session with Randy, I created a new vision board that represented a written description of the physical and emotional attributes I sought in my soulmate. Pictures of men holding women in a loving embrace, of couples being partners coupled with affirming phrases dominated the majority of my board. Daily, I allowed the images to seep into my subconscious providing my mind with new programming. My belief was God would send me "the one" so, I prayed and imagined using the information on the vision board and the list I created with Randy.

God Said, "You Need to Go!"

In the summer of 2011, I met a college friend, Kelly, for dinner at her house in Houston. It was right after a certification training for Zumba, which was my hobby for the three years after my divorce. During the evening, we talked about life and the subject of dating came up. I took the opportunity to tell Kelly and her husband, Scott, that I wanted to date again. Scott quickly responded he knew the perfect guy for me, Donnie. Donnie and Scott were college roommates at Louisiana State University (LSU). He lived in Austin, Texas, and would attend their annual charity party they threw in November called Skotoberfest. Upon leaving their home, a thought crossed my mind, perhaps he could be the gift God would send us.

A couple of months after our dinner, my company re-structured again. This was common practice for major companies after a buyout. For years, we lived in constant fear of losing our jobs. After the 2008-2009 financial cri-sis, they conducted one restructuring after another. As a single mom, it was frightening to think about losing my job, my financial security, and a means to offer my son the health insurance he needed for his asthma. At the end of October, Pfizer announced that my division faced layoffs.

I had a choice; do I allow my fear and need for financial security to dictate my **Action** to stay home or do I trust my God instinct? The opportunity of Skotoberfest proved stronger for me. Despite the fear creeping up, I heard a voice telling me, ***"You need to go."*** This thought persisted for several days. Clearly, I felt God prompting me to go to Skotoberfest and potentially meet the man of my prayers and dreams. Lucky for me, the party fell on a weekend Andres spent with his dad, which gave me time to drive the six hours to Houston, Texas. As I drove down the road, my assurance and confidence grew strong within me. I used the visualization techniques Randy taught me during our sessions to focus on the feelings of the encounter.

Randy gave me the suggestion to step outside of my com-fort zone. After three years of unsuccessful attempts to find the one, he guided me in stretching in the area of relationships. Zumba came into play at this point. By adopting new activities after my divorce, it put me on the path to find him. The curiosity to stay open to new adventures led me to Skotoberfest. My **SOUL Identity** kept me curious, whereas my fear-based **EGO Identity** would keep me playing it safe when Pfizer announced the next round of layoffs, and lure me to stay home.

I remained determined to push past my insecurities and try new things. Seeing and feeling my vision of having a true partnership with someone I loved, propelled me to move forward with my life. My determination saved me from my old identity and patterns! I wanted more than anything to marry someone who loved me and accepted Andres as his own.

Create Your Own Happiness

The last three years were lonely for me. Countless weekends spent either eating alone on South Padre Island or reading books at home because not one friend would call to invite me out. Most of them were either married or in serious relationships, which often meant they hung out with other couples. When I reminded them to call me if they went out, I got the feeling they thought I was too busy because I was independent and they felt like they were bothering me. Not hardly. I sensed the married women did not want their newly single friend to hang out with their husbands.

These experiences taught me a valuable lesson in creating my circumstances to be happy. During this time in my life, I learned how to tap into my internal source of happiness. I found when I left it up to others, I felt unhappy. However, when I left it up to myself, I created my happy. Others could not give me the happiness I longed for. Only I could do it for myself.

Curiosity kept me open to new opportunities as they presented themselves in my life during these years of singlehood. Cooking shows became my pastime, and I enjoyed trying new recipes with my guests. Zumba kept me focused on something other than the pain I felt inside. As a result, I was in the best shape of my life. Never in my life did I dream of being a size two. I exercised seven days a week, teaching Zumba and playing tennis twice a week. By healing myself first, I prepared myself to date again.

When I arrived in Houston, I took a cab to Kelly and Scott's house since they lived in an area unfamiliar to me. There were 200 people inside their home! A scene like this is anxiety-inducing for most people, but for me starting conversations with complete strangers comes naturally. After all, as a high performing person in sales, I did this on a daily basis. At my job, I walked up to complete strangers, started conversations, and asked for their cell phone numbers. My job taught me the valuable skill of connection. It's funny how having a *compelling why and purpose* can drive someone to do what others deem impossible or paralyzing.

People spilled into every area of their home! Alabama and LSU were playing, and you could hear the guys yelling at the multiple TV screens. Everyone drank a beer Scott brewed during the year. I made my way to the beers and selected one of them to try. Little did I know Donnie followed me with his eyes and thought, *I'll find a way to bump into her. She looks young. I hope she's closer to my age.*

Meeting "the One"

Donnie spoke to married friends most of the night and desperately wanted to meet me, but he didn't want to be rude. His friends excitedly revealed they expected a baby soon. He waited a sufficient amount of time. After they left, he strolled around the party to find the opportunity to walk up to me.

While chatting with Kelly in the kitchen, a guy approached Kelly to give her a hug saying "LSU won!" I know I said something to him but cannot remember what. After he went outside, she turned to me and said, "Do you remember the guy we told you about back in August?"

"Yes."

"Well, that's him." She grinned.

"Well, geez! Thanks for the introduction." At the moment a persistent thought went through my mind, *go outside*. I thought, if it's meant to be, he'll walk up to me.

Late into the evening, couples with children headed home. I lingered around, waiting for him to walk up to me. At one point, I didn't think it would happen. In the next moment, someone tapped my shoulder and there he stood, right in front of me.

"Hi, I am Donnie." He looked cute except for the beard he sported, and different from the picture they showed me. The beard didn't quite fit his face, it made him look older.

We talked easily for hours while cleaning Kelly and Scott's kitchen. At one point, I felt his hand reach for mine. He held my hand! The visualization became a reality!

By the time we both realized it, it was 2:30 am. Brad, a friend of Donnie's, who drove them to their house, fell asleep on Kelly's couch. Donnie decided he would escort me to the hotel to ensure I made it safely. On the cab ride, he asked for my phone number, promising to call me soon. Deep down, I still had hope, but since my divorce, many men let me down. A part of me wondered whether he would stay in touch, since we lived hundreds of miles apart. Other questions went through my mind like, *how would he react to the news I had a son? Would he turn and run away like the other men?*

When we arrived at my hotel, he leaned in, wanting to kiss me, but it scared me to give in too early. I made this mistake in the first relationship after my divorce, and I vowed it would never happen again. Donnie ended up kissing my cheek instead and promising me he would call the following week.

The next morning, Kelly invited me over for breakfast. As I drove up to their home, Donnie stood outside with a group of guys. I felt butterflies in my stomach and my hands shook as I maneuvered the car into a parking spot around the corner from their home. A cold sweat broke out underneath my blouse and my breathing increased. I gathered myself inside my car and took a couple of deep breaths. *You've got this girl! Walk up with confidence, like you own the place, lady.* I glanced quickly into my mirror and fixed stray hairs, put a mint gum in my mouth, and chewed slowly to regain my composure. The car door opened with determination and I strutted up the stairs to Kelly's home, where the men glanced in my direction at the sound of the "click, click, click" of my leather booties. We spent all morning talking. Kelly even mentioned to me how uncharacteristic of him to show any feeling towards anyone. They were all shocked at how he followed me around like "a magnet."

By mid-morning I needed to head back to South Texas to pick up my son, and Donnie followed me out to my car then gave a lingering hug. I secured myself with the seatbelt, looked into his crystal blue eyes, and backed out of the parking lot. On my drive back, I blasted 80s music while tapping the steering wheel and singing at the top of my lungs. Thinking about the night before, the way he placed his hand gently on my lower back and held my hand securely in his gave me goosebumps. My mind replayed our conversations from the night before and early morning and I hardly noticed being in traffic and driving six hours straight.

He waited until Wednesday to finally call me. It's true what you see in the movies, people constantly checking their phones, hoping and praying they'll receive the call; it's such a human thing to do. Men ghosted me so many times before, I almost lost hope he'd call. Of course, my phone sat in another room by the time he called. His voicemail sounded nervous and excited all at once.

My Christmas Gift

I planned on having a conversation about my son with him. I replayed the conversation in my mind on the drive back home. He needed to know before this went any further, in case it wasn't what he wanted. I said a little prayer and returned the phone call. Somewhere in the middle of the easy conversation, the "you know a woman of my age, (thirty-six) has a history, it has been three years since my divorce and I have a son" comment came out. Before he spoke, he paused for a moment where I held my breath, waiting for his response and he completely surprised me.

"I already knew. Kelly made a comment during breakfast on Sunday that gave me the indication you had a son." Donnie told me his "dad" was actually his step-dad, whom his mom married after she divorced their biological dad. A good man had raised him and taken care of them. He had been a child of divorce, too.

With the tough conversation out of the way, the courtship continued. We planned to see each other again in six weeks, during which we called and texted for hours at a time. As with any courtship at the beginning, we each took turns talking about our childhood, what work we each did for a living, and details about our lives.

I learned he was born and raised in Louisiana and was the middle child out of three boys each born exactly two years apart as planned. The oldest brother left in his teenage years to live with their biological dad, Sonny, whom the boys rarely saw after the divorce despite living down the street from them. When Donnie talked about this particular subject, I could immediately sense his sadness and at times bitterness towards his dad. When Donnie spoke about his dad I felt closer to him because he trusted me enough to share the deepest parts of him, despite being an introvert.

Wayne, who married his mom shortly after the divorce, was who he considered his real dad. He spoke at length about how Wayne pushed the boys to get a higher education and how he took care of them through his cooking and qualities he admired about him. Though he was already an adult and had moved away to Austin, Donnie was devastated when Wayne was diagnosed with pancreatic cancer. He told me that despite his immensely busy schedule at work as an electrical engineer, he would often take time off to travel to Louisiana to help his younger brother Gary and his mom with Wayne's care. Wayne's death had a profound impact on Donnie's view of what mattered most in life.

Donnie enjoyed learning that I was a first generation American who grew up with two Mexican parents in a predominantly Spanish speaking part of Texas, two minutes from the Mexican border. I spoke about being the oldest of three kids, and about how adamant our father was that we speak only Spanish at home. He knew I attended Catholic schools where I experienced bullying. He learned I had a passion for charity work from the time I was in high school working as a translator to help attorneys in political asylum cases. He understood my **Desire** to teach my young son to have a giving heart. In one of those conversations, I shared about the time I drove my son to Guadalupe's home to drop off clothes and home items after her home experienced major flooding. Andres realized how truly fortunate he was after he saw what humble conditions his nanny lived in. I spoke at length about my faith to him and how my divorce impacted my relationship with God. We saw each other again in mid December and we spent a beautiful weekend together in Austin, Texas. It felt amazing to be in a solid relationship.

On December 24, 2011, in my quiet home in Brownsville, Texas, I enjoyed a beautiful crisp morning, the perfect time to wake up early, drink coffee, and spend time with God. I sat on my couch next to my brightly decorated Christmas tree, reflecting on the last couple of weeks of bliss. My heart felt full when suddenly tears of absolute joy and gratitude welled up in my eyes. I felt the presence of the Holy Spirit all around me.

I asked Him, *Is he my Christmas gift?*

Yes, He whispered from deep inside of me.

For months after the first relationship ended, I prayed to God to send me the gift of love, the man meant for me to love. My faith never left me. I trusted and believed wholeheartedly my soulmate might find me. In this powerful emotional moment with God, He let me know Donnie was *the one.*

The Awkward Pause

On Christmas Eve, He answered my prayers and granted me the wish and **Desire** from long ago. An **Awareness** made its way to my consciousness, *I loved Donnie*. Donnie was THE ONE I searched for all my life. It caught me by surprise. He called in the afternoon to wish us a Merry Christmas. After a brief pause and both of us hesitated, I came very close to saying *I love you*, but in the end, we agreed to talk later. I wanted him to say it first.

On New Year's Eve we saw each other and reflected on the pause on our call over dinner. We met his friends for drinks and he met my colleagues from Pfizer at a New Year's Eve celebration. We both passed our friends' test. On this perfect night we said *I love you*, but he said it first and in Spanish which I found to be totally endearing.

Having a vision allowed me to create the circumstances I **Desired** for my life. It gave my **Subconscious Mind** new programming and a guidance system. By visualizing my **Desired** outcome, I put all my energy and intention behind finding love once again. Visualization and daily conversations with God became my practice, which resulted in attracting Donnie into my life.

When I practice visualization, it works to attract what I **Desire**. Visualization, focus, and faith have guided me throughout my life to achieve what many others deemed "impossible" to achieve. I used the power of my imagination to become number one in the region for Pfizer, and it happened. I pictured being on stage giving a speech to my peers and national sales director, and in April 2009 I stood in front of 300 of my colleagues and empowered them to believe in themselves and their amazing capability to become anything others deemed impossible!

When you create a vision for your life and use the creative aspects of your imagination, you will tap into the genius inside of you and attract what you want in life. Learn to work with your **Subconscious Mind** and it will help you manifest your visions. The key is unlocking the **Subconscious Mind** and using it to its full potential. Once you decide the change is what you seek, vision is a powerful and essential tool for transformation.

Scripture for Journaling, Meditation, or Prayer

Matthew 17: 20 *Truly I tell you, if you have faith as small as a mustard seed, you can say this to the mountain, "Move from here to there," and it will move. Nothing will be impossible for you.*

When has belief helped you manifest what others deemed impossible?

Chapter 8
I Trust in Him

After taking a new birth control prescription, I noticed I was having trouble finishing my Zumba workouts. Unable to link it directly to the new medication, I assumed it must be due to stress from my demanding job. I kept taking the pills despite the subtle warnings my body kept giving me.

Donnie asked me to join him in Louisiana for Easter so Andres could meet his family. As a single mom, this gave me a sure sign he considered marriage. After dating for about four months, Donnie flew down to be with us at the beach. As we walked hand in hand, I jokingly asked him what he would do if I were dying, would he stay or leave me? He of course answered he would stay with me, he loved me. A couple of days later, a pain developed under my right breast bone. It felt as if air was stuck in between my ribcage and it came and went throughout the day.

A day before our scheduled flight to Houston, my mom noticed how pale my face looked and put her head on my chest to hear my lungs. They sounded tight. She insisted my brother needed to be consulted before we boarded a flight to Houston. He picked up my call on the second ring while he made rounds at the hospital. I detailed my symptoms for the past couple of days. He took into account my age, thirty-six, and my excellent physical condition (exercising seven days a week) and diagnosed me with pleurisy, which is common among young people. When I asked him to explain his assumed diagnosis, he described it as an inflammation of the lining of the lung and explained it would be very painful, and prescribed over-the-counter anti-inflammatory treatment.

My mom had a feeling, as most mothers do, that it was something more serious. However, her attempts to keep us from flying fell on deaf ears. Nothing could stop me from flying to see Donnie in Houston. By the time we arrived later in the evening, the pain in my chest became more pronounced. It ached immensely to bend down and pick up our bags underneath our seats as we deplaned. We slowly made our way to the baggage claim area, where Donnie anxiously waited for our arrival. He noticed immediately how pale and tired I looked and commented it would be best to head to the hotel room. After we kissed each other good night, Donnie retreated to the room adjacent to ours. Upon giving Andres a bath and taking my medicine, we went to bed.

At three in the morning a pain, which can only be described as fifty knives piercing my chest, woke me up. The first thought racing through my mind was *Wow, my brother wasn't kidding. This is painful.* Amidst all the pain, darkness, and fear, a prompting came through very clearly and urgently to me.

Lean forward and you will be able to breathe.

That's how I spent the next four hours. It allowed air to fill my lungs and I could take deeper breaths. With each labored breath, I prayed I would make it through the night. I focused on my breathing, on my faith in God, on staying alive for my little boy, and the love in my life. My little boy's breathing kept me alert and distracted from the immensity of the fiery pain inside my chest for the next couple of hours until I fell asleep.

Deep inside of me, I felt uneasiness and somehow knew to stay alert and listen to God's voice. I kept my focus and thoughts on who mattered most to me, chiefly my young son soundly sleeping in the bed next to mine, and Donnie. I remained calm and directed myself to keep leaning forward and to stay in the present moment, where God lives, free from the fear that would likely have rattled me. Looking back now, I know how incredibly lucky I was but I highly recommend calling emergency services should any of you experience this pain. Your focus and thoughts are the key here. Thoughts are incredibly powerful. They will either keep you calm and direct your actions or they will rattle you. Stay on the side of love when faced with a medical issue. Love is where God lives.

You are Lucky to be Alive!

Donnie knocking at our door woke us up. I'd fallen asleep sitting up, which likely saved my life. We called my brother immediately, who upon hearing about the plane ride instructed me to "Get to the ER now and get a CT scan of your lungs."

He insisted, "Don't leave for Louisiana until you have the scan." In all my years of knowing him, I never heard terror in his voice until this call.

The tightness in my chest felt a hundred times worse than the day before, and it hurt to walk or to do simple tasks like putting on my seatbelt. On the ride to St. Luke's Episcopal Hospital, it became evident to me this could be a very serious situation. While Donnie and Andres parked the car, I walked into the ER by myself.

After completing the brief survey of questions, they led me urgently for a CT Scan of my chest. In less than an hour, they conducted several tests to determine the root of my pain.

Five minutes after receiving the scan of my lungs, a critical care pulmonologist walked into my ER room and stated boldly and coldly, "A woman in your condition should not be talking to me right now. You're lucky to be alive! You have two rather large pulmonary embolisms in your left lung."

He explained the sharp air-rending pain I felt the night before was two blood clots that passed through my heart to move to my left lung. There were several others through-out my chest and they figured out I had an inflamed liver. "We'll have to do a second scan tomorrow to determine the cause of it, but for now we will admit you in stable condition on the floor."

They put me on a Heparin drip, a common medicine used to dissolve blood clots. Then my arms turned a blue and black color. It took all my strength and determination to crawl out of bed and walk to use a landline since my cell phone had zero service. I needed to talk with Donnie to explain the situation to him. As any mother would do, I pushed past my pain and focused on my little boy. *What would happen to Andres? Who would take care of him? How will he get back to Brownsville?* The hospital nurses, most of them mothers, understood my plight and intervened.

Why Can't My Mom Come Back With Me?

I finally reached Donnie, who promptly called my brother to explain the situation to him. At first, he didn't want to tell our parents, but I insisted they know. They had a right to know their daughter's medical condition. During all this chaos, I explained to Donnie that Mom could keep Andres calm. He needed reassurance that everything would be okay. Once they notified the staff of the special circumstances, they authorized Donnie and Andres to visit me.

Upon seeing me hooked up to machines, Andres' chin quivered and in a strong voice asked the doctor, "Why is my mom not allowed to come back with me?" As gently as he could, he explained to Andres his mommy would be okay now because she had medicine helping her. It took all my might to not break down in front of my six-year-old little boy. I looked into his tear-filled eyes and told him in a soft voice, "Be strong, Andres. Mommy will be okay since the doctors are taking care of me. Grandma will be here soon." As soon as they were out of sight, I broke down sobbing.

A case like mine baffled them. Rarely did they see it this severe in a young patient. They continued running tests to determine how and why I had developed so many pulmonary embolisms. In the midst of it, my mom texted she was on her way. In this moment it finally hit me how close I hovered toward death, the fear building up all morning spilled out. My heart raced and my breath diminished with each sob. They gave me oxygen to keep me as calm as possible and to assist with breathing. The excruciating pain through each breath felt like I was suffocating, and it terrified me. I kept asking God, "Why is this happening?"

My thoughts during those early hours on Good Friday focused on my son's mental wellbeing and Donnie, who had to choose whether to stay with me or leave for Louisiana to spend Easter with his family. Several times I gently asked him what he wanted to do, to which he always replied, "I am not leaving you!"

He knew the gravity of my condition because he consulted with his brother Gary, a nurse, who explained the situation to him. He wanted me to know his commitment to stay with me every step of the way. The only time he left my side was to pick up Mom and my sister-in-law, who had made it safely to Houston. I can only imagine what my mom felt to see her strong independent daughter lying in a hospital bed with several IVs and oxygen. By this point, my breathing had become increasingly strained. There were times I didn't want to breathe because of the intensity of the pain and heat accompanying each breath. They kept me as stable as possible with morphine for the pain, but it kept me in a constant state of nausea.

The Waiting Game

The doctors were most concerned about my liver and why it looked inflamed. They sent the liver specialist to see me. He explained the blood work revealed very little in terms of information, but they needed to wait until the morning to conduct another test. In his medical opinion, the blood work revealed no cancer, but it perplexed them what other issue could be the cause. While lying in my hospital bed, I kept thinking about my little boy and my fate. *Would I survive this? Would Donnie leave me?*

This situation would definitely put our relationship to the test. Despite the fear creeping up, I stayed calm and faithful. I talked to God, asking him to show me the lesson in this, to help me understand and accept my path. Not once did I blame Him for what happened in my life. He always came through for me when I asked Him to help me. I knew in my heart God equipped me for the things to come in my life.

Early the next morning, Mom and Andres came to the hospital to say goodbye. My sister-in-law was tasked to return him safely to the Valley. I kept it together for him while his eyes revealed sadness and worry.

I reassured him, "Andres, look at me, son. Mommy will be back. I love you. You are my brave boy." I hugged him tightly and kissed him. Locking this moment in my heart and mind kept me determined to face the fear and the truth of my situation. As soon as he left, a tech came to take me to radiology for a scan of my abdomen. I felt a renewed sense of determination. God would guide me, and I held onto the belief this storm in my life happened *for me*.

Within minutes of receiving the results of the scan, six doctors walked into my hospital room. The pulmonologist from the ER the day before spoke first. "Sylvia, we have a problem. You have a large blood clot on your inferior vena cava (the main vein removing blood from your major organs) and it's putting pressure on your liver. If it cuts off the blood supply to it, you will go into liver failure and require a liver transplant. Do you see the three doctors to your right?" I nodded yes. "They are part of the liver transplant team and we have assigned them to your case."

Surrender to God

From my vantage point, I saw my mom, whose face looked lost and confused. Tears seeped out of Donnie's eyes, and I looked at the doctors in complete disbelief. He explained all the doctors spoke to my family, and they all agreed to put me on the more conservative approach because of the severity of my case. Potentially, I risked bleeding out on the table if they tried the interventional route because of the continuous blood thinners. They started me on TPA (Tissue Plasminogen Activator), which is a very strong blood thinner meant to completely dissolve the large blood clot now threatening my life. The way the doctors talked about my condition indicated that I might not survive the night. They didn't look optimistic, and it appeared they were racing against time. The blood clot blocked the outflow of blood supply from my organs which put tremendous pressure on my liver. They told me about the long list of side effects of the therapeutic option. Two that caught my attention were hemorrhagic stroke and DEATH. When they said the word, my mind went blank. God provided me with His protection of the news that threatened to shatter my focus, which needed to be on Him. The only thought dominating my mind, **Surrender to God.** I envisioned falling into God's arms and saying, "I surrender to you God, for this is now in your divine hands." I knew science could only go so far and then there was God. God is all abundant. I knew that the pull I felt to trust Him meant He would lead me to the path of greater joy.

These doctors looked weary in search of a positive prognosis. Being in sales, I mastered the ability to read a room quickly, and their energy said grim. I may not survive the night. As Mom made her way outside my room to make a phone call to Dad, she heard the pulmonologist yell impatiently at the ICU director to give me a bed STAT!

"This girl is going to die if you don't transfer her to the ICU today!"

At hearing those words, Mom collapsed into heart wrenching sobs as a young girl who visited her mom next door came over to hug her. A complete stranger to Mom, she held her lovingly for several minutes.

After a short pause, she asked Mom, "Do you want me to pray with you?"

"Yes, please, I need a miracle."

"Our father who art in heaven, hallowed be thy name, thy kingdom come, thy will be done...." When this young girl determined that Mom had gathered her bearings, she quickly and reassuringly told her, "God is good and your daughter will survive, you'll see."

Mom thanked her and quickly gathered my belongings from the room to join me in the ICU.

He Will See Me

On the ride to the ICU, my mind raced in terrifying ways. *Would I live past tonight? What would happen to Andres, Donnie?* I intuitively knew my life hung in a delicate balance by the looks of those around me. I begged God repeatedly to let me live because my son needed me and Donnie needed me. So many faces stared down at me, all of them working succinctly in the ICU room, preparing me for the toughest night of my life. The team included twenty nurses, techs, and doctors hovering over me. They called in an IV specialist to start the TPA drip. With severely dehydrated veins, it made it difficult to find one which required a highly specialized tech to start it. Every fifteen minutes, a nurse would walk in and ask me a series of questions. They were checking for neurological side effects that could impair my ability to answer basic questions to make sure I did not have a stroke.

During the flurry of activity all around me, my eyes fixed on a pair of black shoes poking into the room, I recognized them as Donnie's. He peeked sheepishly through the door and said, "Sylvia, your Mom and I are here." Those words alone put me at ease instantly. They reminded me of my powerful purpose and my "why" for staying alive.

I felt God's guidance and presence to stay focused on the love in my life. Despite the craziness all around me, I felt the serenity through prayer and stillness. I closed my eyes and used the power of my mind to visualize a joyous outcome, one where I would walk out of the hospital healthy and alive!

As most people can tell you, ICU rooms are freezing. All the equipment and machines needed to stay cool, and both Donnie and Mom were wrapped up in blankets. On the other hand, my chest felt like a raging inferno of heat. My insides burned from the excruciating pain, despite having morphine. They kept increasing the morphine dose frequency, which only made the nausea worse.

Donnie and I were in the early stages of our relationship, and I cared how he saw me. I knew the nausea would eventually be more than I could stand, and I kept trying to signal to Mom to make him leave before it did. He refused to leave my side. It's very humbling to have someone you love see you go through all the pain and everything else with a stay in the hospital. *The mask will be off and he will see me. All of me. The vulnerable me. Will he still want to be with me after all this is over?*

The doctors gave the order of medicine to combat the nausea, but unfortunately, it made me want to go to sleep.

What If I Don't Wake Up?

As soon as the drip began, my veins began seething in pain, and my heartbeat increased. I began to pant, unable to stop the irregular breathing. I didn't know what was happening! The night nurse failed to explain the effects of the medicine before she started the drip. Suddenly I heard her belligerently yell, "Breathe, breathe!" The bright lights dimmed as my heavy eyelids closed.

No! I don't want to go to sleep! What if I don't wake up? What is she injecting into my IV line? Why does it burn so much? The nurse ordered me to close my eyes, to just relax, and even stated angrily that I must be a type A personality. *What if this is the last chance to gaze into his eyes? What will happen to my little boy? Will I live to see and enjoy my happily ever after?*

My body fought to stay awake, the terror seizing every muscle in my body, when I felt a gentle touch on my hand and a soft voice say, "Sleep now, my love. I'll be here when you wake up." And with his reassurance, my eyes slowly closed with the promise of my love waiting for me. Then everything went black.

At two in the morning, my eyes fluttered open. Everything looked blurry at first. The dim yellow lights in the room helped ease my first attempts at fully opening my eyes. The beeps got louder and louder as I slowly woke up from a deep sleep. I attempted to focus on the spot in front of my bed, where I half expected to see a curled up Donnie. I scanned the ICU room for him. When I realized he'd left, my heart sank. I turned to my right and noticed Mom sleeping in the chair next to my ICU bed. She woke up and as soon as my eyes met hers, she instinctively knew my worry and quickly stated, "I sent him to the hotel. I just couldn't leave you."

I felt gratitude to be alive, to move my body, and to be past the threat of hemorrhagic stroke. The hours seem to tick by very slowly. We didn't know whether the therapy dissolved the blood clot. If not, the next more invasive procedure of injecting TPA directly into the clot could kill me. The doctors explained to us that blood thinners posed a significant risk for someone in my delicate condition with multiple pulmonary embolisms. I could bleed out internally.

When faced with the likelihood of death, life becomes crystal clear, and all the silly things we worry about in life become rather insignificant. At the moment, I wanted certainty the most, but certainty is a myth humans create to feel in control of their lives.

My Easter Miracle

Hours later, on what happened to be Easter morning, Donnie came back into my room. A woman with the Catholic Diocese walked in and asked if we wanted to pray with her. "Of course," we replied. We formed a circle and as we were reciting *Our Father* a feeling of love enveloped the room. It was a love so profound and accepting that I knew instantly God was in the room with us. I felt Him cradle me as knowing my prayers had been answered washed over my entire being. I could feel the power all around us, embracing us, and I knew the threat inside me had dissolved. An unconditional love and sense of peace came over my whole spirit.

When she left the room, Donnie turned to me and said, "You felt Him too, didn't you?" Tears welled up in my eyes as I slowly nodded my head yes. The encounter with God left a loving and warm feeling inside us.

Donnie lay next to me and held me close. We cried tears of joy, knowing in our hearts everything would be okay. He gently kissed and held me until the radiology techs arrived twenty minutes later to wheel me into the procedure room to look at the results of the infusion. The nurse who accompanied me into the department said my face looked serene despite the severity of the situation. The look of radiant joy on the radiologist's face ten minutes later told me what I already knew. The threat was over. There was no scarring in my lungs, no trace of the blood clot, or pulmonary embolisms anywhere in my body, which left the doctors shocked and puzzled. They didn't expect me to survive. The diagnosis just twenty-four hours before, Budd-Chiari Syndrome, carried a 20% chance of survival. It is an uncommon disorder that occurs when a clot blocks the hepatic veins which carry the blood out of the liver. The cause of this disorder and pulmonary embolisms that make blood more likely to clot can be oral contraceptives.

At St. Luke's Episcopal Hospital in Houston, Texas, in April 2012, on what Christians call Resurrection Day, God provided me with a second chance at a new life.

Trusting God has served me well in my life since this **Turning Point**. When I truly surrender to the life He wants for me, I gain freedom from fear and feel more joy. I manifest my vision in relationships with others, I make the logical choices for my life, I release the resistance, which sabotaged me for years. When I let go and trusted fully in His path for my life, I lived life fully embracing change with joy in the journey. Truly surrendering keeps me from needing to figure out "the how" in life. In a medical crisis like mine, trusting in Him became crucial to navigating the situation with confidence, focus, trust, **Action**, and purpose.

Spiritual Awakening

This **Turning Point** awakened me from the life of survival and started me on a quest to find my true purpose in life. *What were the spiritual gifts God gave me, and how could I use those gifts in service of others? What else is there left for me to do? What is the soulful purpose God wants me to fulfill on earth?* It changed my perspective on life and forced me to look at it with a more grateful and reflective lens.

My physical, emotional, spiritual, and mental life transformed after my near-death experience. I realized I had been tying my **EGO Identity** to being successful and valuable at work to prove my worth as a mother, as a wife, and as a corporate woman. My belief before this **Turning Point** was if I got *there* then happiness would follow, but it didn't work that way. Despite achieving the highest awards at Pfizer, my life felt unfulfilled and without purpose. I lived a life based on others' expectations of me. Trusting in Him and His master plan for my life led me to become a voice for other men and women in the world—a life I could not envision until I trusted in Him and fully surrendered to His master plan for my life!

This experience woke me up to the true meaning of happiness, the important people in it, and the purpose of my life.

Scripture for Journaling, Meditation, or Prayer

Colossians 3:9 *Do not lie to each other, since you have taken off your old self with its practices and have put on the new self, which is being renewed in knowledge in the image of its Creator.*

In this chapter, God granted me the miracle of a second chance at life. Spiritually, it meant my old self

died on the day he saved me and my new self began the journey to find my divine purpose.

Think of a time when you faced a pull to change the direction of your life. What small steps did you take to begin the change?

Chapter 9
I Am Patient with His Timing

R eceiving the gift of a second chance changed my perspective of life and shifted my focus. Losing my health humbled me and awakened me to the importance of savoring my precious time with family and enjoying life to the fullest. I came so close to losing it all. My journey up until this miraculous recovery was mainly about surviving the trauma from my past, but God wanted me to understand the journey of life was about enjoying and using the gifts He gave me to serve humanity. He used the **Turning Point** of nearly losing my life to awaken me to the journey which would lead me to my divine **SOUL's** purpose. God used my choices to shift my perspective and to interrupt the **Achiever** pattern in my life; the one obsessed with success and achieving to be happy. By aligning to God's purpose for my life, it released me to pursue this new chapter with purpose and freedom. My near-death experience allowed me the opportunity to trust in God's master plan for my life. He was about to teach me His most valuable lesson yet and something a high achiever struggles with, patience.

I didn't want to say goodbye to Donnie at the airport, after spending the entire week together since my hospitalization. Mom ordered a wheelchair for me since I could only walk a few steps and struggled to breathe. For the first time, my seventy-two-year-old mother held my hand to keep me steady as we boarded the plane.

On the ride home, my thoughts persisted. *How would Andres react when he saw me and more importantly, how did this traumatic event scare affect him?* Andres hadn't seen me for nearly two weeks, which felt like an eternity. I longed to hold him close to me and go back to my life as a mom. We went straight to the school to pick him up. He hesitated at the door of the school and slowly made his way into my loving arms. I searched his eyes for any clues to the obvious emotions he felt during my hospital stay, but they only revealed relief. Andres didn't say much when he saw me at the school, and as I hugged him tight, I told him, "You see, Mommy came back. I love you, Andres. Nothing could stop Mommy from seeing you again."

My black and blue marks served as painful reminders of the medication to prevent blood clots, hidden from view. They prescribed Coumadin (a common and older medication used to prevent the blood from clotting) for a year to keep me from having a recurrence. They considered it to be an old person's medication and there I was at thirty-seven-years-old taking it.

A New Normal

The much needed winds of change blew into my life. God used my choice in taking birth control pills to interrupt my **Security Seeker** and **Achiever** patterns. He knew the lessons which He intended for me to learn about patience led me to His path and purpose for my life. What I didn't count on was that for God to reveal my path fully would take more patience than I imagined. Anyone who spent any considerable time with me, knew patience was certainly not my strong suit!

My focus changed dramatically when I returned. I slowed down significantly and work did not consume me anymore. I still worked hard, I just didn't let it take over my identity like before. The love in my life became my top priority and the internal shifts moved me where God **Desired**.

Over the weeks that followed my survival and return to my old life proved to be harder than I expected. My body needed time to heal from the pulmonary embolisms. I wanted to go back to my exercise routine, but my body required patience while I regained more strength and movement as the weeks progressed. My mom stayed with me for several weeks after I returned. She brought so much joy and peace to our lives, giving us a truly wonderful time. I loved having her near me while I suffered inside.

At night, I insisted she sleep in the bed with me. Before I closed my eyes, I feared sleeping alone with my racing thoughts. The obsessive thought persisting through my mind was, *What if I have a clotting disorder and I don't wake up?* This is something I know now as a coach contributed to the worsening of my fearful feelings, which caused anxiety.

It hit me one night lying in bed, just how close I came to losing it all and started me on a different quest. Never once did I blame Him for what happened, instead I asked Him, *Why me? Why did I survive when others die? What am I here to do? What is the purpose of my life?* It catapulted my journey of understanding what role God wanted in my life. Intuitively, I survived for a reason and I knew God would lead me down His path. Unbeknownst to me,

His path would take a longer route than I expected. God needed me to learn the lesson of *patience*.

A Surprise Visit

During this emotional time in my life, my relationship with God strengthened. My journaling practice helped me rely on His guidance and reflect on my experiences daily. It also helped me find the answers I longed to know, for they were deep inside of me. By decluttering my mind of everyday occurrences, I allowed God to come through my pages. This practice took consistency to master. Some days felt harder than others, but by staying consistent with my practice, it became a good habit which impacted my life immensely. I stacked my new habit of journaling one page a day to my habit of drinking coffee in the morning. Every day when I smelled coffee, it signaled my mind to journal my daily page. I now journal three pages or more.

Journaling is a way to declutter your mind of the thousands of random thoughts and allow you to hear His promptings for your life.

As the months passed by, my joy increased with my daily journaling chats with God, and I felt so grateful to Him for saving my life. My birthday in August 2012 held a special meaning to me and I wanted to celebrate it with those I loved profoundly, my parents, Andres and Donnie. Since my actual birthday was on a Tuesday in the middle of the work week Donnie said he couldn't join me because of a previous work commitment. My heart felt heavy when he explained the situation to me. Instead of meeting up on my actual birthday, we scheduled to leave for New Orleans the next weekend to celebrate together. Most of my male friends suspected he planned to propose.

To cheer me up, I celebrated with good friends at Serenity Springs Day Spa on the actual day of my birthday. My body had been through major trauma, and now I needed to stop working and start living a little more. Donnie called me several times during the day. He likely felt bad he could not be there for me. As I paid for all my spa services, I received a fourth phone call from him, which surprised me. It was extremely unusual for him to call so much. In all honesty, it irritated me. My thoughts were, *If you feel this bad, why aren't you here with me?* He seemed shocked I had not left yet. I told him, "It's Brownsville, not Austin. It will take me ten minutes to get home."

We talked on the phone on the ride home and continued talking as I looked through my closet for the dress I planned to wear. Suddenly, I heard a male voice inside my house. My mind could not process who I heard.

What was my brother doing there?

It took several moments to realize it was Donnie standing right in front of me with a huge grin on his face! My heart beat so fast it felt like it would stop. I still held the phone to my ear in disbelief.

He walked into my closet and said, "Surprise!"

We hugged tightly, and that was when I noticed him shaking. It still didn't dawn on me what he wanted to do. Andres followed him into the bedroom and Guadalupe sensed something big was about to happen, quickly grabbed my son and locked the door behind her. Everything happened in an instant and all I remember him saying, "You are my everything. Will you be my wife?" A moment later he knelt down and extended a box with a beautiful diamond ring in it.

Is this real?

After a brief pause, I said, "Yes!"

I walked out of the same bedroom where I spent countless hours praying and pleading with God to send me someone to love, beaming with joy! My heart beat so fast and the happiness spilled out of every cell in my body. Donnie glanced in my direction with so much love and happiness, his smile wide and eyes dancing with delight! Guadalupe greeted both of us with a congratulatory hug when she noticed the bright shining piece of jewelry she knew she'd find on my left ring finger. My son ran up into Donnie's arms and mine, our family complete.

An Uphill Battle Unfolds

Donnie had flown in that morning and called my mom from the airport. He asked if he could come over to shower and prepare for the evening festivities at my parents' house. Mom agreed. He spent the entire afternoon with my parents. Midday, he asked Mom if he could speak to my dad about something important. Mom, sensing he wanted to ask for my hand in marriage, quickly woke my dad up from his afternoon nap. Donnie recalled this meeting rather comically. In the hurried way in which Mom woke Dad up, his hair initially distracted Donnie from the serious conversation he planned. It took him a few moments to compose himself. He proceeded to ask my dad for his permission to honor the traditional Mexican custom. Dad and Mom both said, "Yes, of course." They were happy I found my one true love.

I radiated pure joy the entire night. A new chapter began, and now the reality of a long distance relationship unfolded. Donnie worked as a partner in a company in Austin, and we decided it would be best if I moved to Austin with Andres. During my divorce proceedings, Frank agreed to not place a geographic restriction on me, which meant I could move anywhere with our son.

I needed to apply for jobs in Austin and believed I would easily find one. After all, I'd spent the better half of my life proving my worth and was confident that Pfizer would want to keep me. I didn't realize what an uphill battle I would fight. But God opened other doors for me. Now more than ever, I needed God's help and as always, He showed up in an abundant way!

Several of my Pfizer colleagues helped me identify possible positions in Austin. They checked with their contacts. They wanted me to have my ever after. One of those colleagues, David, sat with me one morning and helped me create my LinkedIn profile. I took a course from a woman who taught me how to elevate my profile and skills in front of managers and send them a cover page with three points of the results I could give them if they hired me. My dilemma, I needed a job with medical insurance for Andres. Even though in the state of Texas, the dad is in charge of providing the medical insurance, Frank and I decided I would put Andres on my insurance and he would pay for it.

Stretching to My Capacity Zone

Applying for every sales job opening at Pfizer in Austin was fruitless. Every one of them told me, "No, you don't have the relationships here." I would smile and tell myself; *I am a highly capable corporate sales professional!* I stayed focused on His timing and process.

God gifted Donnie to me, and He had a vision for my life and path. I applied the Law of the Rubber Band, which means I created tension between my comfort zone and capacity zone by working on goals that stretched me. I stretched out of my comfort zone by cold calling managers I identified on LinkedIn and asking them if there were opportunities in their companies. I stayed focused on this strategy and others during those five months as I actively searched for a job. I learned that when I relied on God's strength, I had it in abundance, and when I leaned into His understanding instead of my own I remained focused on the task before me and believed He was leading me on the path to greater joy. Throughout these months, I created great connections with managers from other companies who I am still connected to today. My determination and drive impressed some of my prospects and several told me they wished they had a position for me. Daily affirmations like, *I am a multiple award sales professional, I will move to Austin with a job, and I can do this,* kept my focus on my goal and was a major component of my success. Every "No" simply reinforced these beliefs in me and allowed me to go on to the next job offering for a sales position.

I remembered something I'd learned from Dr. James P. Gills II, six-time winner of the Double Ironman in thirty-six hours, who said, "I've learned to talk to myself rather than listen to myself. When I listen to myself, all I hear is fear, doubt, lies, and failure. But when I talk to myself, I can tell myself anything I want to. I can feed myself good thoughts of hope, confidence, truth, and victory. I can tell myself; I can do it. When I learned to talk to myself rather than listen to myself, I realized there was nothing I couldn't do!"

Every time I heard "No, you don't have the sales relationships," I told myself, I am a highly skilled Sales Professional with the ability to make connections, I am passionate, tenacious and patient.

After I received my twentieth "No," I sat in my car and sobbed. Positive self-talk or not, my exhaustion finally caught up with me. I'd sent about fifty cover letters to as many managers as I found on LinkedIn, and traveled to Austin early in my quest with the belief *this could be my chance.* Then they give me the "You don't have the relationships in Austin," typical answer. Even after sharing how I had the skill set and the passion to build those relationships to master the job, it wasn't enough. They had a specific candidate in mind and used this excuse.

I learned about this part of the interview process because, as a highly respected and strategic multiple award winner, I was asked countless times by the hiring managers at Pfizer to participate in the early stages of it. The goal was for me to observe and help them decide whether candidates would be a good fit on the team. Despite the setbacks, deep down I believed in myself. I believed in my passion, drive, loyalty, and integrity to thrive at any job I found. What I couldn't understand was how a highly successful, award winning representative like myself did not have a job in an industry to which I'd devoted so much personal time and energy. What was God telling me by closing all these doors?

Just A Number to Them

At a low point, I honestly felt betrayed by my company. I'd given up so much for them and in my hour of need they shut every door in my face. Even my former manager, who I helped during the first seven years at Pfizer win multiple awards, refused to give me a shot. There were two positions open in Austin and despite knowing the skill set I provided, he too kept other candidates in mind and only interviewed me to make it look official. I gradually realized they considered me just a number, and it broke my heart.

What lesson did God want me to learn from all this? I asked, *God, what do you need me to learn?* In prayer, I spoke with Him as though He were right next to me. The words caught in my throat and caused me so much pain. I remember the afternoon as if it were yesterday. Constant thoughts ran through my mind one hot and humid afternoon in November. I received a phone call from Javier, who had news related to a job I had applied for weeks before. We were partners from the start of my career with Pfizer. He worked as a specialty representative from New York responsible for co-promoting Viagra with me. Since 2001, he had been instrumental in my quest for promotions within the company and had guided me to find a job in Austin.

"Prepare yourself Sylvia, there are internal candidates ap-plying for the job at KCI, you know what it means."

Deflated, I headed for my favorite restaurant in Brownsville. I desperately needed a boost in my mood. I ordered my favorite dish, salmon infused with Japanese and Mexican flavors accompanied by fluffy, moist, ginger white rice, lightly sprinkled with toasted sesame seeds. At my pharmaceutical job, I often ate alone. It allowed me the space to connect with my internal dialogue and review the happenings of the day.

After lunch, feeling like I'd exhausted all my prospects, I sat in my car and openly sobbed.

I contacted several people at KCI, a medical device compa-ny, based in San Antonio with a Territory Hospital Man-ager position available for hire. Then I received some news, which caused me concern. Several candidates within the organization were my competition, and I anticipated the usual response. I asked God to guide my words and begged Him to help me with this interview, to help me stand out to them. By surrendering full control to Him, I released all my anguish, frustration and anger to Him and felt free. God clearly knew my **Desire**. I left it up to God to figure out the "How."

Two days later, I received a phone call from a young manager with KCI, Michael. I impressed him with the lengths I went to connect with several high-level managers at his company in a short time, and decided he wanted to learn more about me. He was young, ambitious, and recently promoted. I knew his type from my nearly sixteen year career in pharmaceuticals. He had a strong **Desire** to prove his worth.

An Answered Prayer

The interview went as the other ones before, but he recognized my drive. He knew the position needed an emotionally intelligent, passionate, and resilient sales person. My talent for turning underperforming territories around intrigued him. He did his homework on me too, which definitely delighted me. A former partner of his in the Rio Grande Valley relayed to him about my solid award winning reputation among various colleagues he called. I was the real deal. Finally, Michael said, "Sylvia, you have shown me you have what it takes to get the job done. I need you on my team. Here are the next steps, you'll have an interview with another San Antonio manager and then finally with the Regional Manager."

I walked out of the interview with hope in my heart. *Could this be the opportunity that God had for me?*

When I arrived back at the airport, I called Javier, who connected me with several internal KCI employees. I needed to prepare for my interview with the other San Antonio manager who'd interview me the next day. I did my research on LinkedIn and asked the internal employees questions. They all told me he would give me trouble. He had issues with strong women, let alone strong Hispanic women like me. Many believed the Hispanic district manager carried a chip on his shoulder. I decided I could not lose at my interview. I needed to answer his questions thoroughly, clearly, and respectfully.

At home, I kissed my little boy goodnight, ate a quick dinner and went to work. After a physically, mentally, and emotionally exhausting day, I wanted to rest, but now I needed to prepare. Tomorrow would determine whether I received a third and final interview with the Regional Vice-President. Michael communicated to me they required him to go through another manager as part of their internal process, but he'd already called Garrett, the Regional Vice-President, with his recommendation for my hire.

After four hours of work, I called it a night. My son slept soundly in his bedroom on the other side of the house, but in the pitch dark and quiet of my bedroom, my breathing and thoughts consumed me. I took a moment to say a silent prayer and prayed for guidance, for His wisdom, and for His support. Here in December 2012, I felt despondent at the end of the line. I needed this job to come through and carried an enormous responsibility to do the right thing by my son. We survived and learned to thrive through so much together. I wanted to provide him with a stable home in Austin. His medical issues required insurance. This comfort I could not afford to lose for him. Pfizer blessed us with very good health insurance, and I wanted to continue to support him.

The Trade-Off

The next morning, as I kissed Andres goodbye at school, peace flowed through my heart. Confidence filled me and I stayed very calm. Calm and stress rarely resided together inside of me. I returned home determined to excel at my interview with Mr. Rodriguez. He called right on time. The questions were similar to the ones with Michael, situational questions, which I'd mastered through many years of interviewing at Pfizer. I remained confident in my abilities and answered with honesty and integrity.

He struggled to understand one issue, why an award winning representative would come to work with them at lower pay. He told me he didn't think I would work hard for them because of it. I paused to allow my conscious, non-emotional mind to think logically about the question he posed.

The answer came to me in an instant. I remembered the concept behind the Law of the Trade-Off, which I learned in a John Maxwell Mastermind a year earlier. I asked him if he was familiar with this concept. He said, "No." I proceeded with as much respect as I could muster in the moment. "The love in my life is worth more to me than the $150,000 total income I am earning with salary, benefits and bonuses. I am willing to trade my six-figure salary and established career to accept lower pay, and start over again as long as I can move to Austin to marry the love of my life and begin my life there. If you give me this chance, I will work harder to prove I am the right candidate."

He paused for a long time, and then he said, "Okay, Sylvia, I'll make my recommendation to Michael. You'll hear from us by the end of the day."

By midday, I received a phone call from Michael, explaining he scheduled my next interview with Garrett in two days. They were eager for me to start in January with the new training class. At my last interview, I knew I couldn't mess up. I convinced Mr. Rodriguez. Hope filled my heart that this could actually happen before 2012 ended.

I made my arrangements to fly to San Antonio, KCI headquarters, and rented my car. I remember sitting in it and praying before my interview. In the quiet space, I envisioned the outcome of the interview.

Garrett would tell me, "Welcome to the team!" My thoughts were with God in the one hour I spent in the car praying and meditating. As I stepped out of the hot humid car in December 2012, I felt a peace come over me. I walked into headquarters with a smile on my face and determination to close this interview with a resounding "Yes, you are hired!"

An Out-of-Body Experience

Little did I know, Garrett, a newly appointed Regional Vice-President, determined he needed someone with skill, experience, and swagger to step in and secure what KCI had in Austin and to grow the territory. I needed to embody a self-motivated, driven, coachable territory manager who took the initiative to educate myself so I'd contribute value instead of consuming it. Garrett, a tall and soft-spoken leader with a genuine smile, couldn't have any missteps considering the situation KCI faced with important customers. He explained to me they required a person with a solid track record of success, with consistent results leading to promotions and advancement. They were in a precarious position with some of the major systems in Texas.

I felt his energy the moment I shook his hand, and it reassured me somehow. I remained calm and ready. He made the interview a pleasure after so many months of stress and pressure. The conversation flowed easily during the hour we were together. How refreshing to encounter a Regional Vice-President who genuinely cared about the people he led. During the interview, I felt a presence take over my words. It felt like I watched from outside of my body and at the end, while I closed Garrett for the territory manager position at KCI. I knew the Holy Spirit filled the room with the feeling washing over me, "Don't worry, I've got your back."

Garrett smiled the entire time. At the end he said, "Welcome to the team, we're so happy to have you join us!"

For the second time in my relationship with God, I felt His providence. God provided me with strength and intervened in the interview in the way He knew Garrett would positively receive the message necessary for him to offer me the job. This experience reinforced my **Desire** to continue surrendering to God all my worries and seek him in my daily life.

I shook his hand and said, "Thank you for giving me a chance. You won't regret it." He instructed me to fill out some additional paperwork for them, which I did. I managed to accomplish what others deemed impossible for the third time in my sales career. I beamed with pride and I couldn't wait to call the three most important people to me, Andres, Donnie, and Mom.

My hands shook from the excitement, attempting for the second time to dial Donnie's number as I stood outside. Donnie picked up immediately. I pictured him anxiously awaiting the news. Tears streamed down my face and emotion caught in my throat as I spoke as clearly as I could.

"I got it!" I exclaimed, as I jumped up and down like a crazed teenager outside of KCI Headquarters in San Antonio, Texas.

The months while I searched, Donnie contemplated moving to Brownsville, Texas, if I couldn't find a job. Donnie received the news with relief and immense joy.

"I cannot wait until we move you and Andres to Austin! I love you and am proud of you! You did it!" We quickly made plans to move my things to Austin.

My Dream Manifested

On the plane ride back home, I allowed myself to cry tears of joy. The five longest months of denials and frustration were over. God used all this to teach me a valuable lesson of patience in His timing and His master plan for my life. I have struggled with patience since my childhood. I always wanted to skip the process and move on with life or the next event. This particular time in my life taught me the value of patiently waiting for the opportunity to secure a job. Humility became my greatest teacher. It humbled me to be told "no" so many times despite the many accolades accumulated in my career. All those accolades meant nothing next to the abundance received in return for my patience. I moved to Austin to marry the love of my life and start our life together with Andres. My dream came true after years of praying for the privilege of love. God granted my **Desire** in a bountiful way. Grief and loss taught me to rely on my vulnerability as a strength to carry me through life's challenges. My hands trembled as tears streamed down my face. A deep sadness and heaviness fell on my heart the morning I sent my resignation letter to

Pfizer. My company of the past twelve years did not fight to keep me. What a painful and difficult realization to come to understand. I was a number to them, a means to an end. All the years spent building relationships, growing my territory meant nothing, after all. What do you expect from corporate America?

As I sat in the empty and quiet house, you could only hear the clicking of the keyboard on my computer as I typed. Javier joined me by phone. He lived in San Antonio, Texas and stayed in contact with employees and tipped me off to an available hospital account job with KCI. His support in my professional journey over the last eleven years influenced me to hit send despite my initial hesitation. Javier gently encouraged me, "It's time Sylvia, send it." I took a deep breath, Donnie's face flashed in my mind, and on the exhale, I hit send. My twelve years of hard work, commitment, and loyalty all left in one tap of a button. I secretly hoped for a job with Pfizer all along, yet in the end, God guided me to other open doors. He knew my destiny and dissuaded me with every "No" from going down the wrong path for my life.

I continue to reap the benefits of the lesson of patience, especially on the journey as an entrepreneur and business owner. God knows what you and I need to learn before equipping us with what is to come. Patience took center stage throughout my transition from corporate sales professional to stay-at-home parent only a year and two months later. This proved to be the most challenging transformation of my life. However, patience would guide me to stay faithful to Him and His vision for me. God will lead you down a path of greater joy and purpose when you stay patient in His timing.

Scripture for Journaling, Meditation, or Prayer

1 Peter 5:6 *Humble yourselves, therefore under God's mighty hand, that He may lift you up in due time. Cast all your anxiety on Him because He cares for you.*

Journal about a time when you waited patiently for things to work out the way they were meant to. How did patience serve you and your interests?

Chapter 10

I Receive God's Blessings with Love

G od's blessings abound when you invite Him to actively participate in your life. I looked around and grasped at the enormity of this moment in my life. It represented many feelings to me, happiness, sadness, joy, and pain. I walked to the family room and a rush of memories flooded me. My little boy took his first steps where I stood. As I looked at the vast backyard from the family room, I remembered all of my son's birthday parties and the fruit trees I planted as a hobby. I peeked into my son's playroom next to it and remembered the day Frank asked for a divorce as Hurricane Dolly pounded the coast. I walked outside, the sun shining brightly and the air crisp. What a glorious morning!

As I made my way to the side of my home, the memory of my thirty-fifth Spanish themed birthday party flashed in my mind; my parents sitting on outside tables enjoying Sangria and Paella, and my guests fanning themselves with a fan they received as a favor. Around one-hundred guests celebrated my single-hood in style as Spanish Flamenco music blasted from the outside speakers. I looked out the window of my office, which overlooked the patio, and remembered many quiet moments in solitude on the weekends while Andres stayed with his dad.

Hello Austin!

Back inside, I made my way to my bedroom. The baby picture of Andres stirred many precious memories. A friend of mine, a photographer, took it while I held him. As I prayed to God, this portrait reminded me of the privilege of love after my painful divorce. Joy filled my heart as I stepped into my closet where Donnie proposed. The emotions flooded me, and I dropped to my knees to thank God for my life. All of it had been worth this moment. Hope, love, and strength permeated my insides. Jesus filled me, and I knew He remained in control. In two weeks the movers would neatly pack all of my memories and my life in boxes.

On a crisp morning in January 2013, I stood outside my home. We packed my company car from KCI to the rim.

Andres wanted to ride with Mom, who took half of the boxes. Mom would be with Donnie and Andres for the next few weeks unpacking the house and ensuring Andres a smooth transition to our new life. The company expected me at headquarters in two days to learn all the skills I needed to join surgeons in the operating room. Guadalupe and Rosie, the two nannies who had helped me for the last eight years, sobbed as they held my son in their arms one last time. My son looked scared and sad. The move would take us away from our friends, our family, and our home.

It was a major **Turning Point** in my life, and I felt scared and happy all at once. Six-year old Andres felt happy because he loved and trusted Donnie but very sad and scared because he loved his school and friends and knew he would be in a brand new school after the Christmas break. He wondered when he would be back to see everyone, especially his dad. The divorce decree did not contain clear language or direction, it only stated no geographic restriction. I wondered, *How will this land with Frank, once the reality hits that Andres now lives hundreds of miles away from him? Will he be a present or absent dad?*

We drove a couple of miles and when I looked in the rearview mirror, I saw the last seventeen years of friendships, Sundays with my parents, early morning coffee with the nannies, my successes as a pharmaceutical representative fading in the distance on a cold, dreary January day in Brownsville, Texas, and I cried. I said goodbye to my life as I knew it, and hello to my new identity.

Mom joined me on the phone. I could barely speak between sobs, and she told me as gently as she could, "It's okay, Sylvia. You are making the right decision for your life. Your dad and I will be okay."

I felt selfish for wanting a better life for me and my son. It felt like a betrayal to my parents and to the nannies who depended on the work I gave them to survive. They knew the entire story, and they witnessed my pain and sorrow for so long. They celebrated when Donnie proposed, and they understood it was time for me to move on.

God blessed me with a fresh start on the life He envisioned for me, a gift of love and I, his faithful servant accepted it as I drove the hundreds of miles to our new life which awaited us.

The next two grueling weeks at the KCI training were nothing like I'd experienced before. My exhausted mind struggled to learn so much anatomy in a short time. Selling medical devices turned out to differ greatly from my previous career, and was like pharmaceuticals on steroids.

Fast paced, action packed, and highly stressful days kept me away from my family for two weeks, but then, KCI gave me some time to reunite with my family.

We met in San Antonio for a fun-filled weekend! I made Andres my top priority and couldn't wait to spend time with him. Although he loved spending the extra time with his "Ita," short for Abuelita, my mom, who he adored, he wanted to spend time with me. The weekend fueled me with the energy needed to continue for the final week at KCI headquarters. When the time came to leave, tears welled up in my eyes, and I hugged them all goodbye. I knew what I needed to do, and yet all I wanted at the moment was to go home with them.

Joy Awaits You on the Other Side of Fear

Mom stayed behind with Donnie to help care for Andres and take him to school during the tough transition. Andres struggled to adapt to his new environment. His teacher often called to say he had issues at school. He erased his answers obsessively, answered questions literally, and blurted out during class. His Attention Deficit and Hyperactivity Disorder (ADHD) and Obsessive Compulsive Disorder (OCD) were apparent even then, and I missed it. I attributed it to the stress of the move to a new city, home, and school. My little boy experienced trauma when I became ill and spent weeks in the hospital. Then came this move months later. It triggered his anxiety and the ADHD and OCD showed up to give us clues to his mental state.

In retrospect, the signs were all there. However, we missed it because we were busy adjusting to a new school, preparing for the wedding, and a new job. I wanted to give it time to see if he'd settle in before I took him to a doctor. It was a mistake to allow shame, and fear to play a role in my decisions.

In retrospect, I now know the old belief systems were clearly in control. In my overwhelm, my **Security Seeker** pattern kept me from exploring his issues with a psychiatrist. I made the mistake of allowing society's stigma on mental health and the shame associated with mental health in Hispanic culture to dictate my inactions. Fear took me down the longer path to joy.

It's important to interrupt these patterns when they show up. Joy awaits you on the other side of fear, when you have the courage to step into uncertainty, with faith despite not knowing the final outcome. I made the mistake of reverting back to old patterns because it was comfortable to do so. It's how the **Subconscious Mind** works. It takes daily intentional conscious work to interrupt thoughts that fail to align to who I could become. Looking back now, I see that in my excitement, and busyness of my new life, I momentarily lapsed from engaging with God as I was doing prior to this change. As a result, my fear was doing the majority of the talking in my head and it led me down the wrong path.

Unbeknownst to me, my hospitalization triggered my own anxiety, which is genetic in our family. Unfortunately, I modeled obsessive hand washing, overthinking, and over-reacting to my young son without being aware of it. Modeling matters. My child took cues from me to guide him. The healthier approach to this situation would likely include seeking the help of professionals earlier, incorporating meditation to create new neural pathways, and most importantly keeping God at the center of my life.

In the research I've done since then, I've learned a great deal about this prevalent issue in our society. Anxiety can be genetic and is likely triggered by a traumatic event. It can be exacerbated by the modeling kids experience from their parents too. God sent me several messengers like Dr. J.P. Moreland, who conveyed all of this to our congregation during his talk on anxiety. He wrote a book which I read to further understand how to change the neural pathways through meditation. I learned new ways to address it to help our family manage this genetic condition.

God Delivers

This job required me to be in the operating room with surgeons, and I had so much to learn. However, nausea overcame me at the sight of blood, a fact I concealed from my employers. I prayed to God the night before my first surgery. He knew what I needed and trusted He would guide my **Actions**, words, and focus. Surprisingly, as the surgeon made the first cut with his scalpel in hand and the first draw of blood, my early queasiness dissipated. The smells and sight of blood no longer bothered me. God delivered!

From a vantage point outside of the sterile area, I guided the surgeons on the use of the Wound VAC, a medical device which suctioned the bacteria and helped close the surgical wound over time. My customers loved this amazing piece of advanced technology, but it needed improvements.

Amputations, grafts from burn victims, and the smelliest, most disgusting bacteria infected wounds you will ever see up close became my daily routine. Only by a miracle from God, I never passed out in surgery or in a patient's room!

Maintaining my focus helped me throughout those first few months in my new role. My mindset remained strong and determined to deliver the results I promised Michael and Garrett. My previous experiences at Pfizer were instrumental in my success at KCI. The lessons in passion, perseverance, and patience served me well in my role as hospital account manager. I knew it would take time to develop relationships with the key players in those accounts. My ability to make connections easily coupled with my confidence allowed me to stretch the rules to accomplish my goals within the account. In my previous job, I walked into the hospitals without appointments. My strong connections with nurses, pharmacy departments, and nursing directors had been instrumental in my success. I applied the lessons learned at KCI and developed solid relationships with the surgery technicians. They were key players who recommended the use of them to the surgeons and ensured my advancement.

Conflicting Parenting Styles

On the home front, it took time to adjust to living with Donnie. I was used to being the parent in control of my son's discipline. The guilt I carried over from the divorce drove my need to protect Andres more than was needed. In my mind, I shielded him from harsh discipline at the hands of Donnie, because I felt he required more affection after the many changes he underwent; whereas Donnie felt he needed more structure and correction. In his mind, I excused him when he crossed boundaries with me. An example would be when Andres talked back to me in a disrespectful tone and I would allow it by arguing with him instead of imposing an immediate consequence.

On the other hand, Donnie, grappled with his first crash course at being a parent while vacillating with the precarious balance of discipline and affection. He only knew how to be Andres' friend and not his father. He joked around with our son by making mean comments like boys do to and with each other but when Andres would joke back, Donnie would pull the dad card. Another matter complicating their transition, was Andres' inattentiveness and blurting out when Donnie helped him with his math homework. To Donnie it came across as lack of respect, when in reality it was the early symptoms of his ADHD. Consequently, after multiple interruptions, Donnie would lose his patience and yell at Andres. I would often intervene during these exchanges and we ended up fighting. We both failed to set up healthy God-centered communication at the beginning of our marriage and allowed our pride and stubbornness to guide our **Actions**. These conflicting parenting styles confused our son and created resentment.

My job's grueling twelve-hour schedule contributed to the **Emergence** of ingrained patterns of achievement to rear their ugly heads. The release of new products at the time of my hire, meant longer hours and little leeway for error. I felt compelled to deliver the results I promised them during my interview. But somewhere deep inside of me, a battle began once again. My **SOUL** longed for a balanced life of love and family and halfway through my employment the realization hit me, this job was the wrong fit for the woman I was becoming.

Work, Avoid, Control & Repeat

God prompted me several times to slow down. He wanted me to fully enjoy my new life in Austin, but I reverted back to consulting with Him when times were dire instead of engaging with Him daily. I wish I could tell you that my newfound clarity and drive to find my divine purpose guided my **Actions**, but that would be a lie. I had yet to create the **SOUL Identity** of someone who knew how to invite more joy into her life by being the person God envisioned me to be. The truth was my **EGO Identity** of workaholic and **Perfectionist** was well ingrained into my being and I unfortunately fell back into old **Habits** of work, avoid, control and repeat. It's what I knew. Life moved at a faster pace. It was easier and less tiresome for me to feed these patterns instead of interrupting them to create new joyful **Habits**. This was completely normal to do and it happened because I failed to roll up my sleeves and work through my pain and create the identity of someone who receives gifts from God with joy. Had I released my need for control and security and asked for His help, it would undoubtedly have helped me navigate this transition faster. At times I felt abandoned by God, but I left Him out. I stayed too busy achieving to be happy instead of happily achieving.

We each came into the marriage with baggage. Our lack of **Self-love** also played an enormous role in the relationship struggles we experienced at the beginning of it. I happily gave my love away, but I didn't feel worthy of receiving it. I felt I had to earn it, because of my relationship with my own dad. Donnie grew up with a mom who failed to give or show affection as well as a dad who practically abandoned them. These traumas hurt our relationship in our early years together. I allowed disrespectful interactions with him, despite Mom's repeated advice to set up healthy boundaries from the beginning. We certainly took the difficult road to arrive at the place we made it to in our relationship today! When you invite God to participate, you'll make the loving choices to serve you. He sees your beautiful **SOUL** and wants you to have abundance, love, and happiness!

Despite the stress of our jobs and adjustment struggles, we still managed to focus on the love we felt for each other. We spent our weekends finalizing the details of our wedding and spending time together as a family. Austin, Texas is an epicenter of fun family activities, dance halls, and music festivals! With a plethora of things to do, we had an amazing time discovering our new home. The wedding details were the fun part of our relationship. I thoroughly enjoyed browsing different sites to create the rustic chic look we wanted.

A week before our nuptials, we received a summons to appear in court in South Texas. Andres' dad wanted to establish a different visitation schedule, and he waited until the last minute to file the paperwork, no doubt intending to ruin our happy day together. What a poor, vile attempt on his part to hurt me. Luckily, our good friend Scott worked in a prestigious law firm in Houston, and Donnie reached out to him for advice.

Scott immediately jumped into action and referred me to a colleague of his who is known in lawyer circles as "one of the best" in their profession. God definitely stepped in to send messengers my way. Scott and his colleague were our angels, providing sound legal advice which led me to hire a fierce woman attorney, Jan Cassidy, in Harlingen, Texas. Everybody knew Jan for her integrity, hard work, and resilience. Despite my repeated attempts to pay Scott's colleague, he refused to accept payment, later admitting he felt compelled to help me. God's gifts abound when you receive them with love!

God's Blessings Abound when You Receive with Love

Jan stepped in quickly and filed a motion to extend our court date, giving me the necessary time to focus on my marriage and honeymoon.

She told me, "Sylvia, go enjoy your special day! I've got this!"

With a deep sigh of relief, I released my feelings of resentment attempting to rear their ugly head. No way would I stand for my ex-husband's miserable attempt to destroy our joy. Returning my focus to the beautiful week ahead with family calmed my heart. My aunts and uncles from various parts of Mexico arrived a couple of days before the Saturday of our nuptials. Good friends from around the country flew in to witness my ever after in the most beautiful venue in Austin, Villa Antonia. Donnie's family from Louisiana came and spent time in our home. His younger brother Gary, the best man, gave an entertaining toast at the rehearsal dinner which made everyone burst out laughing. Even his father, whom he had a distant relationship with, came a couple of days to help transport guests to our wedding. We organized transportation to and from the venue for our guests, and set up everything needed for our big day.

The obstacles I encountered during this dynamic year in my life taught me a valuable lesson in receiving God's blessings with love. No matter how tumultuous life gets, there are always pockets of joy that God gifts you along the way. God needed me to learn how to receive His gifts for He knew what I needed to flourish into the person He envisioned me to be! God, once again, used these **Turning Points** to remind me that He is always there to help when I seek Him with all my heart.

Scripture for Journaling, Meditation, or Prayer

Ephesians 3:16-19 *I pray that out of his glorious riches He may strengthen you with power through His spirit in your inner being, so that Christ may dwell in your hearts through faith. And I pray that you, being rooted and established in love, may have the power together with all the Lord's holy people to grasp how wide and long and high and deep is the love of Christ, and to know that this love that surpasses knowledge that you may be filled to the measure of all the fullness of God.*

God's love was evident in this chapter. As this scripture points out, God's love for you is so wide, long and deep that when you feel it you know He is with you and will bless you with His glorious riches.

Reflect on a time when His love for you was evident, despite the hardships you faced. How did God show His love for you? Who did He send as His messenger(s)?

Chapter 11
In Faith, I Thrive

After so much pain and sadness, I remember feeling elated with my dream of love coming true. The day of our wedding arrived, June 14, 2013, and typical for Texas we endured the scorching heat of the sun while the sky radiated blue with a few clouds dancing across the sky. What a contrast from the night before, when a cool breeze blew across the balcony and allowed us a sweat free rehearsal.

We finally made our way to the venue, Villa Antonia, an old-world-charm, Mediterranean home nestled amongst the breathtaking landscape of the Texas Hill Country. A hair stylist and makeup artist met us there to prepare for our special day. The bridal party arrived hours before us and waited to help organize the bridal and groom quarters and be available for whatever came up. The bridal coordinators dispatched one of the bridesmaids to bring a fan to place underneath my wedding gown to cool me down. Luckily, they chilled the champagne and tequila to pour the minute we arrived. The festivities started fairly early, customary of a true Mexican and Cajun party! We arranged our photo session before the ceremony to not impact the party after our wedding and had drinks throughout. The photos we took seemed relaxed and fun, which is what we wanted to create for our bridal party and guests.

Donnie knew how to make me feel beautiful, simply standing in his presence, the way he looked at me with so much love and tenderness. My little boy beamed with excitement to celebrate with his cousins and my parents, who were all in town to help us celebrate.

As I ran around getting ready, I noticed the worried look on my sister's face. My best friends, Cassie and Andie, sat with me. Kelly, my best friend from college and Scott's wife, stood nearby, too. I could sense Roxy knew something. I broke the ice and suspense by asking very calmly, "What's up, Roxy?"

She replied, "Our brother is not coming."

My brother promised to walk Mom down the aisle. My friends and family couldn't believe he didn't let us know sooner, except me. I felt a peace come over me at the moment and I matter-of-factly asked, "Well, who can walk Mom down the aisle?" I went directly into action mode. Everybody who knew me could not believe how calm I stayed in the moment. After deciding quickly to release my feelings to God, I chose to focus on my joy at the moment. The joy gave me happiness for the day of my wedding. Nothing could shadow the love I radiated inside. Years before, a situation like this would consume my attention and overshadow my joy. Since my near-death experience, I learned to leave my worries in God's capable and loving hands. My uncle Juan, my mom's older brother, perfectly filled the job and felt honored to participate in my wedding. Everything worked out as it should all along.

I stood at the top of the winding outside stairs, waiting for my song cue to slow walk down. My gown, light ivory and strapless, clung tightly on my waist. For a brief period, I allowed myself to savor the moment with the scent emanating from my bouquet of English roses. Tears of joy suddenly appeared, and I thanked God once more. My heart overflowed with gratitude for His gift of love in my life. Then in the distance I heard the first tempo of the song we'd rehearsed the night before and I took the first steps down the aisle. My daddy waited for me at the bottom of the stairs, rose petals scattered by the flower girls along our path. Our guests smiled warmly. Our officiant, Judge Jan Breland, was a funny and kind person, and I knew from the moment I met her that she would be a special addition to our wedding. Our groomsmen sweated profusely under the Texas sun, as did some of our guests. Oh, the joy of June in Texas! As miserable as they looked physically, I sensed their joy. Donnie waited a long time to find his happily ever after too.

Leveling the Playing Field

Halfway through the ceremony, Judge Jan took out her handkerchief and wiped the sweat off of Donnie's face, which made everyone laugh. We'd written our vows. I went first and then Donnie. As Donnie vowed to love me, he momentarily lost his train of thought. I looked deep into his eyes and smiled brightly. I could sense he forgot some of what he meant to tell me and looked mortified. "It's okay. It's just me." Almost on cue, he remembered and finished his thought.

Then came my favorite part in the ceremony, the exchange of rings with Andres. Donnie picked out a silver ring, which he gave our son as a sign of his commitment to him as well. Our families each took a rose then put it in a vase symbolizing the unity of our families, a beautiful gesture to include in our wedding.

After our wedding, we spent a few days with family before leaving on our honeymoon to the Grand Cayman Islands. For a brief period, we relaxed into our new life together. Jan Cassidy, my attorney, managed to extend my court date until October. She prepared our case by countering with an increase in child support payments. She explained we could use his lawsuit to our advantage. A new law in Texas stipulated child support could increase to $1700 a month when they earn $100,000 or more a year. She liked to use this strategy to even the playing field.

The court assigned us a judge who favored men in visitation cases. This knowledge added to a level of stress in my life. Not only would I have to fly down to Brownsville on several occasions missing work and my home responsibilities, but I needed to prepare emotionally and mentally for a judge known to hand out judgements giving men the upper hand in court proceedings. Wonderful.

Jan kept me sane during this stressful time in my life. She researched and responded efficiently to all communications, which increased from Andres' dad. Whether I wanted it or not, change rushed into my life once again. There were two choices from my perspective. I could stick my head in the sand and dwell on the negative in my life, or I could change my attitude about it. There is always opportunity in the challenges life gives you. You have choices.

Extending an Olive Branch

Luckily, several other hospital managers at my company could step into my cases to ensure continuity, to give me time to savor the honeymoon and the start of our new life. Meanwhile, KCI wanted me back in the game as soon as I arrived from our honeymoon. My work gave me a way to channel the pain into something fruitful.

I found it rewarding to encounter new opportunities for growth, especially in my work relationships. Veronica, my partner in wound care facilities, and I battled with compatibility from the beginning. The tension between us since my start at KCI became noticeable and felt by all who encountered us together. This set up an opportunity to stretch outside my comfort zone. Taking the lead to resolve our issues, I invited her to lunch. She waited for me outside at one of the picnic tables. I placed my food tray on the table and with an outstretched hand said, "Nice to meet you, Veronica. I am Sylvia." She smiled nervously and tentatively reached out to shake my hand. I told her, "I've noticed you and I don't really get along, and I'm wanting to understand why?"

Veronica responded, "Well, I feel tension between us too."

"Let's talk about it then. The way I see it, we need to help each other out. We can be a better team if we understand what's going on."

In the course of our conversation we both realized our manager, Michael, inadvertently created tension between us by sharing too much information during the interview process. Veronica competed as a candidate with me for the job I received. I know he meant well, but his competitive spirit sabotaged him and our relationship.

My mistake was failing to reach out to Veronica, and set up a meeting in the beginning. Sometimes in situations with others it's best to clear the air at the start. Being in growth mode, because of dealing with my ex-husband, I decided to change my environment at work with the partners to ensure growth continued. From the moment we closed the gap, we became unstoppable as a team at KCI. Today, we remain close friends. When Veronica turned forty, we took a couple's trip to Jamaica to celebrate it with Veronica and several other friends.

Will I Be Able To Carry Our Baby?

At a time when most newlywed couples our age would naturally have a baby, we consulted with multiple doctors. Doctors explained to me at St. Luke's Episcopal Hospital the possibility of not being able to carry a baby due to the complications resulting from the pulmonary emboli episode. When we arrived in Austin, I found a Hematologist to run a series of blood tests on me to determine whether a genetic predisposition to develop blood clots caused my problems. My internist took me off Coumadin, the blood thinner two weeks prior to the blood test to ensure an accurate reading. In the meantime, we communicated with my OB/GYN and considered multiple options, including surrogacy. Donnie dreamed of having a biological child of his own, and I wanted to carry our baby.

As we sat there waiting for the results in the Hematologist's patient room, Donnie took my hand in his and we said a silent prayer. After what seemed like ages, she confidently walked into the room where we waited for our fate. Dr. Shrikhande was a kind-hearted physician with a calming bedside manner. She looked into our anxious eyes, smiled warmly, and said,

"You guys look so worried! There is nothing to worry about. Your tests came back negative for blood clot disorders, which tells me your birth control pills caused your pulmonary emboli last year. In the interest of being thorough, we'll need to see Sylvia every year to run these tests again." She patted both our hands and said, "For now, you can stop taking Coumadin. You cannot take any hormone therapy ever though, so regarding a future pregnancy, you will need to be on blood thinner therapy to carry your own child. I have many patients with your situation, Sylvia."

She gave us both a smile and a wink and left the room. We both seemed to breathe for the first time since she walked into the room. God answered our prayers and dreams.

We called my OB/GYN's (Dr. Michael Phillips) office the moment we stepped out of Dr. Shrikhande's office to set up my appointment. Dr. Phillips, shared the best news. I could carry a baby as long as Donnie injected Lovenox shots into the skin of my abdomen during my pregnancy. He began injecting me from the moment we decided to try for a baby. They were painful, but my husband kindly reassured me through his steady hand. Needles terrified me, and I shook every time I tried to give them to myself. The injections left multiple black and blue marks on my belly, which was common with blood thinners.

Time to Move On

By December 2013, we were expecting our first baby. Our miracle realized rather quickly and caught us both off guard. Life continued its busy pace while our joy intensified. To be pregnant at thirty-nine gave me a newfound reassurance that all would be well. Donnie and I kept it a secret for a while and spent Christmas at my parent's home looking radiant with joy. After so many months of worrying, I carried our child.

The job at KCI turned into an issue between Donnie and me. He grew tired of my late nights and early mornings. My family hardly saw me. I resented my job immensely because it took the joy out of my everyday life. In January 2014, we traveled to Nashville, Tennessee for his company's Christmas party, and for the first time Donnie took me to one of his parties. They were eager to meet their partner's new bride.

On the plane ride there, a plastic surgeon and I had an intense confrontation over the phone. He wanted me in the hospital helping him with a device which failed in surgery and demanded me to solve the problem for him on a Saturday. I respectfully explained I was out of town with my husband and offered to give him the number of a partner of mine. He refused and said I was responsible to show up. I called my manager, Michael, who offered to help the physician out himself.

With every interaction it became clear, I needed to look for another job. I wanted a conducive environment which provided joy in my life. Stress threatened my pregnancy. We could enjoy ourselves for a brief time in Tennessee, but I retired early, no doubt exhausted from my pregnancy and the argument with a physician who threatened to take business away if I didn't help him myself.

At thirty-nine years old and pregnant for the second time in my life, the argument with the doctor proved to be the last straw. It made me realize work would always be there. The important people in my life mattered more to me than the job or great benefits. When I returned from Nashville, I was determined to create a new life with our family. I resigned from KCI on Tuesday, February 4, 2014. A huge weight lifted the moment I hit send. My heart reassured me, I made the best decision for myself and our family. In an hour, we would see our baby on screen and I could hardly wait!

Donnie encouraged me to stay home while I decided what to do next. In the meantime, he would put Andres and me on his medical plan. I honestly don't know why we didn't do this from the beginning of our union. It certainly would have made the transition smoother and less stressful. As a single parent, I had grown accustomed to being in charge of all aspects of my child's wellbeing. And as a woman and mother, I also struggled to ask and receive help.

Just When Things Felt Like They Were Falling into Place

We drove in separate cars, because he needed to go to a customer's site after our appointment and I needed to round on patients at North Austin Medical Center afterward. I gave KCI a two-week notice, and planned to leave everything in order before I left. We walked into the appointment with our hearts full and happy about having a child together to expand our family. Dr. Phillips greeted us. He is an Austin College graduate like me, and we fell into easy conversation while he put the jelly on my stomach to perform the sonogram. He kept moving it around, and a worried look came across his face. I sensed it immediately.

He said, "Guys, I have bad news. I don't see a heartbeat. I'm so sorry." My eyes filled with tears, and Donnie sat in shock. Dr. Phillips squeezed both our hands and gave us a moment to be alone. Heartbreaking sobs filled the room the moment Dr. Phillips stepped out of the room. Donnie's entire body shook silently as his head hung low. He dreamed of having a biological child for so long. It devastated me to watch the love of my life break down as he stared at a sonogram with his baby who didn't have a heartbeat. At two-and-a-half months along and at my age, with my medical history, this loss defeated both of our spirits. Why did my dream seem so out of reach?

With heavy hearts and broken dreams, we walked out slowly, with our shoulders drooped, to my car. Somewhere deep inside of me, I knew instinctively my baby died in Nashville. I felt sick after dinner and very weak. No doubt the stress from my job contributed to our loss. Alone in my car, Donnie openly sobbed for ten minutes. I held him in my arms while I took my turn to be the strong one. When I knew he could listen, I held his tear-filled face in my hands and gently kissed him. I said, "It's okay. We can try again."

After his car drove past me and out of sight, I allowed myself to lose it for the first time since the news. A cold shiver went up and down my spine as my body shook un-controllably from my sobs. My vulnerability in full display. My gut instinct told me to call my partners Veronica and Nadia. They needed to know as soon as possible. I could barely catch my breath when Veronica picked up. Worried for me, she asked, "Honey, what's wrong?"

In between sobs I managed to utter, "I lost the baby, Veronica."

"Where are you?"

"Near North Austin Medical Center," Over the course of the last four months, Veronica became a close friend.

"Let it out. It's okay. Do you want to meet for breakfast?"

I said yes. I needed to be with people, especially good friends. We decided to meet halfway between North and South Austin. Just like multiple times in my life, I wiped away my tears and focused on what I needed to do to move on from this loss. My family needed me to be strong. *It was just a setback,* I thought as I started my car. I hugged my midsection and quietly said, "I'm sorry, baby. I'll see you in heaven."

Why Suffer Alone?

Veronica and Nadia were amazing. They listened while holding my hand throughout the conversation.

Veronica, being the logical one, said "Maybe, it's a good thing you aren't pregnant right now with flu season. It may be God's way of protecting you. There are hardly any beds available in hospitals with the surge of cases right now." She always had a way of making me feel better. They both understood my need to step down, especially after what happened with the plastic surgeon. They ensured I was okay before they left to finish the day's work.

Mom called me in the afternoon, completely unaware of the day's events. They wanted to come see us and wanted to know if it would be okay for them to come up on the weekend. God quietly worked behind the scenes. Through tears welling up in my eyes I replied, "Of course, Mom, we would love to have you." God sent us angels to help with our grief.

Dr. Phillips advised us to include our family in our news of the miscarriage. He said, "Why are you guys going to suffer alone at a time like this?" We thought about what he said and decided to tell our families about our loss as soon as Mom and Dad arrived. They came to comfort all of us, for Andres took it especially hard. He'd dreamt of having a sibling from the moment I met Donnie. And now at home we sat down to tell him. As a family we put our arms around each other and wept. I know we will one day meet our baby in heaven. I trusted God would lead me to the path of greater joy. My faith sustained me while I grieved the loss of our baby. Despite the enormity of my circumstances I held onto the belief that **everything is happening for me and not to me.** Changes in your life and dreams challenge you, but your faith comes in to help you grieve. Have faith and remember everything is happening *for you*, and not *to you*.

Andres needed to see my vulnerability, as did Donnie. In our vulnerability, we find our strength to continue putting one foot in front of the other. Life's journey is full of moments, opportunities to see life through a different lens. With faith in God, I believed he would give us another sweet baby. Veronica made a good point about the timing being off. God's timing is perfect, and we do not always understand it. I've learned to lean on His understanding and not on my own.

Before they put me to sleep for the dilation and curettage, (D&C) the procedure I needed to prepare me for another pregnancy, I looked into Donnie's crystal blue eyes and smiled, "I'll see you when I wake up." That's the last thing I remember before everything slowly faded away.

Grief & Loss Became My Greatest Teachers

My broken heart covered me like a wet blanket of sadness all weekend, but my mom and dad provided relief. We played cards to distract us momentarily from our grief. Donnie, the den leader of Andres' Cub Scout group, took him to an event. We were grateful to God for the blessings of our friends who dropped in with food to comfort our **SOULs**, and for the activities to keep us preoccupied and busy.

Grief and loss were my greatest teachers. In one year, I lost my job at Pfizer, my life in Brownsville, and our baby, but I gained a beautiful new life in Austin, a great deal of wonderful friends, and the opportunity to have another baby with Donnie. Now, I'm reminded how my focus helped me experience loss through a different set of eyes. In looking back on this time in my life, I am grateful for the lesson in faith God taught me.

Faith allowed me the freedom to step into an unknown world of uncertainty, and this stepping stone in my journey of self-discovery equipped me with the necessary foundation of **Self-love**. I made the loving choices by starting over in medical devices, and marrying Donnie instead of getting caught up in the what ifs and staying with a company that did not value me. By stepping out of the carefully crafted box of perfection, I ventured closer to the woman of faith I was always meant to be. In faith I thrived despite the circumstances threatening to derail my joy.

Scripture for Journaling, Meditation, or Prayer

Hebrews 11:1 *Now faith is confidence in what we hope for and assurance about what we do not see.*

How has faith sustained you when circumstances fail you?

Chapter 12

I Accept My New Path

As we waved to my parents goodbye from our front porch and the car slowly pulled out of the driveway, a knot caught in my throat. My body shivered underneath my black wool coat as I tugged my hands deeper into its pockets to keep the chill from seeping into me on that cold, gloomy day. The little girl inside of me screamed, *Please don't leave me. Please stay, I need you!* I wanted to run after my parents and escape the pain which threatened to rip my heart in two. *Lord, please give me the strength to endure this loss.* My eyes welled up with tears as I crumbled into Donnie's warm embrace.

From Corporate Woman to Stay-at-Home Mom

The first two weeks after the D&C procedure proved the toughest to endure. Donnie dove into his work with a vengeance, no doubt his way of channeling his pain, but I felt lost without a job as my escape. For the first time in my adult life, I held no paying corporate job, which required my attention. *What am I going to do for eight hours while Andres is at school?* In spite of the fact my own mother had been a stay-at-home mom, I was completely inexperienced at being a homemaker. Our home filled with silence during the day, which drove me completely nuts because I was used to the grind of fifty to sixty hour work weeks and the noise of working in hospitals. Being **Action**-oriented and successful came naturally for a type A like me. I mastered the art of succeeding over the first half of my life. And now time and silence filled my days. These served as God's tools to chisel away the unwanted layers of trauma, doubt, unworthiness that created beliefs of *I'm not enough unless I achieve* and *my success is determined by the size of my paycheck.* He wanted me to see myself as He saw me, worthy, gifted, and blessed.

As with any change, the beginning is always the hardest to move through. I gained my footing with each passing week and soon began to create a new schedule to give my life structure and purpose. One thing I loved about my corporate job was the people I got to see and talk to on a daily basis, which this new venture did not provide. My friends all had nine to five jobs and limited time to chat. On my list of to do's was to find a group of moms and get the 411 of this new life.

Losing the baby left me with a gaping hole, so I filled my time by volunteering at Andres' school and joining a tennis league to inject a little joy to combat the grief I felt inside. The leagues welcomed me with open arms. They needed a singles player on their team, and since I played singles on my college tennis team, I fit the mold. The television served as an entertaining vehicle for me to immerse myself into while I folded laundry or washed dishes. Music provided my aching heart with a dose of joy when waves of grief hit it.

Donnie did not understand how much pain I truly carried, because I chose to mask it with a smile. *How could he understand my broken heart if I didn't include him in it?* This is a common mistake in women who have a habit of pleasing people. They hide their pain from others and suffer in silence.

What often happened to me when I avoided pain was I dove into hobbies as a distraction. Tennis became my outlet to everything I felt inside. Not only did I deal with the heartbreak of losing my baby, but I felt lost in my new normal. I sought answers outside of me instead of looking inward for them. I tried to figure out the "how" instead of releasing it to God, which would have allowed me to savor the small moments of joy with my son and husband. Part of me felt I betrayed my baby by feeling joy too soon, an often occurrence for anyone journeying through grief.

God's Intended Purpose

People advised me to take a break, even my husband said, "Go and play tennis. You need a break, you've worked hard for so long, Sylvia. You deserve it." I played so much, I hurt my left foot which required me to wear a boot for months. God clearly used my choices to shift my focus back to Him. After being sidelined from tennis by the injury, it encouraged me to engage with my life and to turn to Him for advice.

Perhaps Andres' au pair announcing her intention to leave our home in a month came as a blessing in disguise. God used these choices to refocus my energy on Him. The purpose He intended for me to fulfill in my new role required my full attention, therefore, He sent my mom to guide me, for He knew her influence over me. Mom called me often. In one of our daily conversations, she told me, "The body knows, Sylvia. You'll soon have a baby. Focus on your new life at home with your family." Somewhere deep inside of me, her words gave me hope. Mom always spoke words of empowerment to me. My decision to rely heavily on my internal source of wisdom to guide my new life showed me the answer.

Our faith remained strong in us, regardless of the deep, searing pain of our loss. Every Sunday for months, we drove forty minutes to a church a couple of friends recommended would lift our spirits. One brisk and crisp morning as Donnie parked the car, I hobbled over to a bench close to the entrance and sat down. On the drive over, despite the happy chatter in our car, my mind took me back to our last sonogram visit. I struggled to keep my composure intact the whole way there, afraid of openly sobbing in front of Donnie and Andres. Safely alone amidst a crowd of people, I allowed myself to collapse on a chair, completely exhausted from the emotions and the short walk it took to arrive at my seat. My eyes filled with fresh tears and my heart sank as the memory of Donnie in my arms came into full view. My poor husband, I thought. *What did this loss do to him? How can I help him cope? I wanted to give him a gift of life. Sylvia, you need to stay strong for him, and for Andres. God, please help us, please help my body carry our baby, keep us safe from harm.*

On cue, God sent an angel to me. One pastor who frequently filled in sat down next to me. He asked about my boot and we fell into an easy conversation. Deep inside my core, a voice said, *Tell him.* In a moment of vulnerability and heartache, our story spilled out of me. No doubt he felt my despair, guilt, and doubt. God knew my heart, and He sent a messenger to give me faith.

He listened intently while his assuring blue eyes never left mine. When I finished our story, he leaned in and put a gentle hand on my shoulder and said, "Let me pray for you. Lord, please give Donnie and Sylvia strength and the will to continue their path." Just then, a tingling sensation filled my whole body. A protective shield of love embraced us and peace came over me instantly. God would bless us with a child soon. For the first time in three months, I felt joy and hope. Just then, Donnie and Andres walked up to us. Donnie, the perfect gentleman, extended his hand and helped me up. Slowly and lovingly, we all walked into the congregation together as the Christian rock band played our favorite song.

The Lies I Believed

Once the excitement of this new transition died down, the new normal proved harder than imagined for me and

Donnie. It affected our dynamic immensely. Donnie felt more pressure and responsibility to be the breadwinner. The at-home career shift proved a drastic change for someone like me who felt more comfortable working long hours and getting paid in exchange. At the heart of my **Limiting Belief** lived the lie *I am not enough*, which tied my value as a human being to the amount of money I brought to the table. The thoughts of *"What is my value now if I wasn't getting paid?"* dominated my internal dialogue. Clearly, God needed me to accept my new path and the lesson He intended for me to learn. I wish I could tell you I fell easily into this understanding but my **EGO identity** stepped in to wreak havoc. I psyched myself out even before I started the transition, because of my lack of **Awareness** of the power of my subconscious programming and its influence on my mindset.

My view of the stay-at-home mom role, coupled with the modeling I received as a child, further reinforced my resistance to accept my new path. I saw this lifestyle as a luxury for moms to stay home and take care of the house. Plus, as immigrants our parents taught us at a very young age, our worth correlated with being successful. I carried around an immature way of regarding the important role moms play in the lives of their children. Conflicting societal views fogged my focus. I remained stuck in recovery mode instead of acceptance. Instead of leaning into *His understanding,* I leaned on my own.

My stress caused multiple health issues to arise shortly after my resignation from KCI. Both Donnie and I required the removal of suspicious looking moles on our backs. It turned out they were in early stages of melanoma. What a blessing to discover them when we did. Shingles developed on my throat, an extremely painful and embarrassing issue. It felt like one health issue after another popped up. However, when you allow stress to accumulate, the body will attack, and mine certainly took aim at me. Within a three-month span, all the negativity purged out of me as God prepared my body. He needed all my issues resolved before He blessed us with a baby. In late March 2014, we found out about God's blessing for us at seven weeks pregnant. Luckily Donnie and I resumed the Lovenox injections six weeks after the D&C procedure, to prevent blood clots. Just as before, when I lifted my shirt, I saw the black and blue marks appear at each injection site, but all our effort proved worthy in the end. I knew God would bless us with love in **His timing**.

A Baby Girl Is On Her Way

My pregnancy went smoothly. My skin glowed, my hair held a radiant shine, and my joy was felt by all who encountered me. When the pregnancy made it past the first trimester, Donnie exuded happiness and relief. God granted my wish with a baby girl on her way to us. I vividly remember the day of the gender reveal, tears of joy filled my eyes, and I thanked God for the gift of Vivian. Friends celebrated with us by organizing baby showers in Austin and Brownsville. Everyone cheered with joy for our little family as bliss filled our lives for several months as we prepared for her arrival. Our home overflowed with gifts and her room transformed into a palace worthy of a little princess, compliments of Restoration Hardware and Donnie's amazing ability to make everything beautiful. The setting was now perfect for the much anticipated arrival of our little girl.

Andres joined us for our five-month visit. His eyes lit up and he grinned the moment he saw his baby sister on screen. He truly embraced this new adventure after his visit. He excitedly told everyone at school his little sister would join our family soon. No one could miss our happiness.

It seems now, in retrospect, God prepared me for our next adventure. He gave me the gift of time with my kids and family, and a prayer answered. I see it now, years later, but then my **Subconscious Mind** steered the helm of my **Actions**. I failed to see the gift. My belief that *I am unworthy* lived at the core of my attitude, focus, feelings, and ultimately, **Actions**.

The Protector & Provider Emerges

Now as a sole breadwinner, Donnie felt compelled to work and provide for his growing family. His company depended on his expertise immensely and my husband, being a solid man guided by integrity, felt compelled to deliver. My king made great strides to build his castle for his queen, prince and soon to arrive princess, only I didn't understand it at the time. He worked long hours at his company, and gave 150% on the job. His need to protect and provide caused a great deal of stress in our house, as did my habit of picking fights before he left. From my point of view, it felt like Donnie didn't want to be with us when he refused to stand up to his partners and communicate his **Desire** to be a present dad and husband. In my mind, he deliberately ignored my **Desire** to raise our family together. But oftentimes, the anger shows before the sadness which lies at the heart of miscommunication and lack of connection between spouses.

My resentment grew when I found myself alone a great deal of the time. What further poured salt on this deep wound, was my belief that I was the second choice. This drove my habit of picking fights and as a result we engaged in battle. I acted on feelings of unworthiness which developed early in childhood. My dad worked long hours and rarely stayed home. As a young kid, I felt second best to my dad's job as a doctor. When my husband worked long hours and traveled for work, my feeling of unworthiness surfaced. Instead of incorporating healthy communication by vulnerably sharing my positive need to him, I resorted to criticism.

Both of us had our own perspectives and feelings we were operating from and unfortunately our communication and connection took a hit. When it was evident to me that Donnie did not intend to slow down, I focused on the joys of my pregnancy and Andres' activities at school to fill my days with fulfillment.

Finding My Tribe

As anyone who transitioned from the workforce to stay-at-home parent knows, it takes a little getting used to this new role. To adapt to my new surroundings, I reached out to friends at Andres' school for advice and guidance. Parents we met at Cub Scout organizations be-came our friends. Donnie and I stayed heavily involved in Cub Scouts at Andres' school. He continued serving as Andres' den leader and I held the advancement chair position for several years.

I met Valerie and Alana at school events. They talked to me about the transition they made from corporate life to being stay-at-home moms. I saw a light at the end of the dark tunnel. They advised me to create a structured week by assigning days to laundry, shopping at grocery stores, paying bills, cleaning the house, etc. One perk, they enjoyed lunch out once a week. This sounded like the best medicine for my ailing heart. Val, as most people called her, was pregnant with her third child. We instantly connected, and both of us were expecting baby girls and her husband was the nephew of a wonderful friend of my father's. God sent Val to me. No question about it, for He knew how tough this transition would prove to be for me.

During a Cub Scout event at our school, Val introduced me to a couple of the ladies from PTA. They spoke about their need for a president. By the way they discussed the matter, it appeared no one wanted the job. Honestly, I don't know what compelled me to volunteer, but I highly suspect my *Succeeder* pattern emerged to channel this need to be valuable.

I Need to Earn the Right to Have Joy

For years, I tied my value to the size of my paycheck. If I didn't produce one, then it meant I brought no value. It was all or nothing. With this transition, I realize now, God wanted to remove these layers of **Limiting Beliefs** and **Habits** I formed over the years as a response to the significant emotional events of my life. He wanted me to learn the lessons of **Self-love** and self-worth by seeing and loving myself as He saw and loved me. My value lived inside of me, only I focused on the outside achievements for it. Deception hit me in the head and clearly in my delirium I accepted the new role.

My flaw as the **Succeeder** was to find success from outside sources like the PTA instead of turning inward. My loss of identity as a corporate woman fed this pattern. To fill the void the loss left in me, I turned to this perceived opportunity to provide me with the confidence I needed to find my way. The **Succeeder's** flaw is failure to be honest with themselves. They find success elsewhere. Seeking it from outside sources becomes their quest to fill in the void of the painful circumstances they face. Lack of confidence and courage lies at the root of their dismay.

No one else wanted the job, and I soon found out why. My decision surprised Donnie and scared him for me to take on such a stressful role while pregnant. He knew my values of integrity and responsibility would propel me to go all in. The role at PTA satisfied the need to feel valuable for now, instead of savoring the time God gifted me to enjoy life more.

Something inside of me felt the need to earn the right to have happiness in my life. It likely stemmed from the generational belief in Mexican culture that women had to sacrifice something in order to have it all. A woman couldn't enjoy her children and be a corporate woman. It was one or the other but not both. Achieving happiness and significance by being a top performer at my corporate job filled the void of unworthiness. Attention, affection, and appreciation of others in my previous role gave me the significance I secretly craved.

If only I'd understood then what I know now.

Your worthiness exists inside of you, not outside. No job or relationship can ever give you the fulfillment

and happiness you seek, only you can do it for your-
self!

What therapy sessions and a joint coaching session years later uncovered was that my need to feel appreciated and seen by my husband was at the root of my drive for significance. I turned to outside sources to provide it for me instead of just communicating it to him in a positive way.

What further caused undue stress in our marriage, was my need to emotionally connect with Donnie by sharing my hardships and challenges encountered at PTA. He listened to *solve the problem* which is a common way men listen. As a woman I needed to be *listened to and understood*, not fixed.

After an OB/GYN visit a couple of months later, Dr. Phillips gently yet sternly suggested I step down. My blood pressure shot up high on the visit. With the medical history of pulmonary emboli and my forty years of age, my pregnancy was classified as high risk and geriatric. Every week they monitored my blood pressure to avoid complications.

When Closed Doors Become Blessings In Disguise

God closed another door to guide me to Him once again. In September 2014, during a PTA meeting, I announced to the board my intention to resign. My relationship with God became my source of comfort and solace. My friends, Val and Alana, who served with me on PTA, invited me out to lunches to encourage me and it worked. I leaned into my new life and prepared for the new baby who graced us with her beautiful presence three months later.

In December 2014, a beautiful vivacious baby girl with sparkling blue eyes and golden hair made her way into our world. Donnie took three months off work to help me take care of her. He gladly took the night shift while I took the early morning feedings. Mom came for a month to help us with Andres and baby Vivian. We spent three glorious months together as a family of four. Our dream was finally realized with the birth of our baby girl.

With her birth came a renewed sense of responsibility in Donnie. Even though the owner of his company suggested Donnie enjoy his time off with his family, he insisted Donnie take on extensive travel upon his return three months later. In his absence, the company struggled. They realized Donnie played an invaluable role in the productivity and efficiency of it. Unfortunately, throughout the years, they'd become accustomed to relying on Donnie to re-solve ongoing technical issues with difficult customers.

A month after Donnie returned to work, we traveled to Louisiana for Easter. Donnie never took all of his vaca-tion at his company and knew he still had some left to use. A surprise waited for my husband when we arrived in Louisiana. I'd secretly organized a surprise family re-union/birthday party for him. Members on both sides of his family united for a day of barbecue and outside games at a state park near New Iberia. Everyone met Vivian for the first time. We spent a beautiful weekend together as a family and it was the last vacation my husband took that year. Upon our return, he worked extensive hours and the strain of raising two young children keeping our house op-erational and managing our newly established real estate business he left entirely up to me.

It seemed his travel schedule increased dramatically after he returned to work. I think deep down he felt pressured by his boss to work unachievable hours to make up for his time with Vivian after she was born. His two identities, **EGO** and **SOUL**, began their inner battle. But eventually his **EGO Identity** of **Achiever** stepped into center stage.

On the home-front, I dealt with life alone with the kids, the operational upkeep of the house and the management of our business. The constant grind triggered postpartum depression, which went undetected. Many nights I dealt with low self-esteem, emotional issues I thought I buried long ago and unresolved issues with Donnie. We lacked true partnership and understanding of each other's plight. It was in this dark place, I sought solace in God. I found his loving voice on my pages as I consistently journaled page after page of daily occurrences, fights with Donnie, and joyful moments with the kids. God sent several angels to protect me and provide me with the answers I needed to move forward in acceptance of His timing and ways.

Acceptance of My New Path

This year presented us with many transitions. Our **EGO Identities** steered our actions more than our **SOULs** did. We both made mistakes by viewing our plights through our lens instead of our partners'. Was it our intent? No, that's why it's vital to invest in personal growth and seek God's guidance. Doing it has helped me unlock the secrets and lies my **Subconscious Mind** held within me. I felt the Holy Spirit present in me and I tapped into His wisdom when I felt stuck in my relationships with myself and Donnie.

Learn to communicate honestly and clearly from the beginning of your relationship with your spouse. When life kicks your relationship down, seek outside help.

There's zero shame in this. It's best to understand your spouses' motivation and how they like to receive love. In my husband's case, listening to *understand,* and acts of service brings him joy. For me, words of affirmation and appreciation fill my cup. We both walked into our marriage with tons of baggage and expected the other to accept it. Our past set us up for failure, because we modeled the toxic behavior which others modeled to us as children. He modeled emotional **Detachment** displayed to him by his mother and father, and I modeled self-worth tied to achievements my father taught me. Marriage is certainly not for the faint of heart. It takes work from both sides to ensure it's successful. Love is worth it in the end. Do the work.

I've always known in my heart, God put us together for a powerful purpose. Donnie's work provides me with the security and confidence to do God's work. My attitude towards his work and self-worth was my failure. I secretly resented his success and lost my joy along the way. I realized my problem involved me tying my self-worth to my performance at work. The lessons He intended me to learn were that my self-worth comes from Him and I must accept myself as I am. He created me to be a part of this beautiful world and shine a light in the darkness.

Self-worth supplied me with joy. To operate from this state freed me to give love and receive it in return. When challenges threatened to derail my path to become an author, I stood on the foundation of this lesson to keep me on my intended way to do God's work. It helps me be a better mother to my two kids. Acceptance of the purpose God has for my life liberated me to enjoy the creative process of writing in complete partnership with Donnie who as provider worked in conjunction with me to realize God's master plan for each of our lives. My value was so much more than the size of a paycheck. It was in the love and guidance I gave my kids, it was present in the messages God commissioned me to give my community. My life and every transition I've been through served an immense purpose in transforming lives and relationships.

It's a privilege to share my mistakes, failures, triumphs, and lessons with you on these pages. If one life is transformed by this book, I've fulfilled my purpose as an author and coach.

During the writing of this chapter, God spoke to me about the role He wants me to fulfill. He led me to the books of Jeremiah, the weeping prophet, and Huldah, a prophetess. I also participated in a twenty-one-day Angel Adventure class which led me to the Archangel Gabriel, a messenger of God. Prior to Covid, my church identified one of my spiritual gifts as prophecy. God's preparation for this time in my life took years and lessons in between. I needed to accept my self-worth from within and tie my purpose to His.

Scripture for Journaling, Meditation or Prayer

Luke 22:42-43 *Father if you are willing, take this cup from me; yet not my will, but yours be done. An angel from heaven appeared to Him and strengthened Him.*

In this verse, Jesus is asking His father for strength for the physical torture He knows He will endure with His crucifixion.

Think of ways God has shown up in your life to provide you with the strength to accept His will and not yours.

Chapter 13
I Am Authentically Me!

O ne morning as I openly sobbed on the phone with my mom, she gently encouraged me to seek counseling.

"You need someone more qualified to guide you, Sylvia. Your balance is off, my love."

Her words comforted me and I began my quest to find a therapist who could unlock the reasons behind my sorrow. God gifted us with a beautiful baby girl, and I couldn't seem to shake this feeling of sadness. *Life was beautiful. Why couldn't I see the joy? What was wrong with me? I loved my husband and family and* **Desired** *to stay married. My marriage was worth it. I was worth it.*

After calling around, I scheduled an appointment with Cynthie Grace, a counselor who specialized with helping women. I quickly fell in love with her style of therapy and the space she offered. Art work decorated the walls, the lavender scent calmed me instantly, and the warm lighting kept me calm along with her quiet and observant demeanor. She listened intently as I poured out my heart to her, periodically jotting down notes on her yellow legal pad. Her insightful questions guided my **Subconscious Mind** to reveal the truth. I felt heard and safe to share my story with her. After a couple of sessions, she recommended the book and TedTalk, *The Gift of Imperfections* and *The Power of Vulnerability* by Brené Brown.

True to form, I googled and listened with curiosity and openness. It helped me clarify what Cynthie intended for me to understand. My need for perfection with its sidekick shame robbed me of the joy of life. Brené spoke into my **SOUL** and I realized I lacked belief in my worthiness of love and belonging. The self-talk definitely needed to change, as did my **Self-love**. I found it easier to treat others kindly and with compassion, but when it came to doing the same for me, I fell short. My strive for perfection masked my unworthiness. I needed to release my need to achieve, and embrace the authentic me. Only I didn't know her yet. I faced an identity crisis. The expectations and lies my **Subconscious Mind** fed me were at the core of my confusion, and I chose to believe them as my truth.

I didn't know how to live in the now where joy existed. Either I lived in my past or anxiously obsessed about my future. I longed to discover what held me back from experiencing love. In sessions, we discussed how to reprogram my self-image and treat myself with love and compassion.

Brené Brown described perfectionism in *The Gifts of Imperfection*:

Perfectionism is, at its core, about trying to earn approval and acceptance. Most **Perfectionists** were raised being praised for achievement and performance (grades, manners, rule-following, people pleasing, appearances, sports). Somewhere along the way, we adopt this dangerous and debilitating belief system. I am what I accomplish and how well I accomplish it. Please, Perform, Perfect. Healthy striving is self-focused—How can I improve? Perfectionism is other focused—What will they think (Brown, 56)

Perfection is an illusion you create to feel in "control" of your circumstances. Anytime I felt overwhelmed and out of control of my circumstances, my **Perfectionist** Pattern operated under the surface to help me cope. However, the time came to release it lovingly. Time to uproot it and shift to worthiness and love. Time for me to love myself so I could model it to my kids.

During my weekly sessions with Cynthie, we focused on **Self-love**. She helped me see the gifts I held inside of me, left untapped to their true potential. She determined my compassion and vulnerability God gave me to share with humankind. Then she planted the seed of self-discovery and encouraged me to write a book. I knew my answers lived deep inside of me, waiting to surface to my conscious **Awareness**. I longed to discover what held me back from experiencing **Self-love**.

Discovering Me Again

I grew closer to God during this quiet time in my life and wrote in my journal daily. The act of visualizing Jesus as if he were sitting right next to me helped my connection strengthen. God answered my prayers by prompting me to reach out to certain people and to his angels, to help along my journey of self-discovery. One afternoon, I called Humberto. I met him many years before and hired him to take my first wedding photos. Shortly after my divorce, he took pictures for my thirty-fifth birthday celebration and other special occasions. Since then, he became a life coach and guided me well. His wisdom reflected the many books he read and his training, and life experiences added layers to his guidance. A voracious reader, he constantly recommended books for me to read. One afternoon, we spoke at length about my identity crisis.

As usual, he listened intently and gently encouraged me to work through *The Artist's Way,* by Julia Cameron and journal three pages daily to declutter my mind.

He told me "Even when you don't feel like writing, write this line over and over again, I don't know what to write, I don't know what to write, I don't know what to write...trust me all it takes is one time you do this and you'll be cured and write anything on your mind." In my case, it never happened. This gave me the structure to begin my daily self-care ritual of journaling to connect with God. I sporadically connected with God and by implementing the morning pages, I established a routine which yielded amazing results and connection with Him.

Humberto recommended I work through her book slowly. I took only what spoke to my **SOUL**. The Artist Date resonated with me. In essence, it's what Julia describes as taking yourself on a date, only you, once a week. She recommended you make a list of all activities which illuminate your **SOUL**.

Julia Cameron described an Artist Date in *The Artist's Way*:

The Artist Date is a block of time, perhaps two hours weekly, especially set aside and committed to nurturing your creative consciousness, your inner artist. In its most primary form, the artist's date is an excursion, a play date you pre-plan and defend against all interlopers. You do not take anyone on this artist date but you and your inner artist, a.k.a your creative child. That means no lovers, friends, spouses, children—no taggers—on any stripe. (Cameron, 18)

My creative side waited for me to discover it. The answers I sought within me would emerge from morning pages and artist dates.

My **EGO** attached itself to my corporate past life where achievements, success, and my value tied themselves to accolades and significance from others. Anger, frustration, doubt, and lack of clarity clouded my way. *Did I make the right decision to transition to become a stay-at-home parent?* An internal struggle between my fearful **EGO** and **SOUL** ravaged my insides. *Who the hell was I? What was my purpose?* I felt like I lost so much of myself, my life, my work, and part of me resented Donnie for it subconsciously. My whole life, I'd known my path and my direction. When I lost my way, I felt like a failure. The truth would be found when I empowered my **EGO** and embraced my **SOUL** (God's vision for me and inner wisdom) and they operated as a cohesive unit instead of two separate identities.

Only God could empower me to shift my fearful **EGO Identity** from a space of doubt to a space of joy. My foundation was built on fear, perfectionism, achievements, and significance. When the transition to be a stay-at-home parent occurred, it crumbled all around me. I needed to fully surrender control to God and His master plan to be whole. It was time to rebuild my foundation of love for God, for myself, and for others. It called for letting go of my need for approval from anything outside of me. I needed to give myself love first. Only then could I truly step into the transformative process God was preparing me for all these years of patiently waiting for my divine purpose to emerge.

The problem became my **EGO**, the self-image, which operated from a foundation of fear and blocked me from being able to receive and give love to myself. It's okay to grieve the loss of your old life; just watch out for prolonged periods of grief which can lead to the resistance inside of you persisting longer than it needs. This determines whether you created a habit around your grief and whether you are avoiding pain by not working through it.

God sent angels to guide me on my intended path to help with the inner struggle I experienced and the loneliness I felt being in a city with few to no friends. My good friend Val suggested I join a baby music class at Brushy Creek Community Center. Wednesday became my new favorite day of the week. For one hour, several moms and dads would meet with their babies to participate in a hands-on music class. I met Kathryn, who quickly became my closest friend in Austin. One afternoon she approached me to ask if I wanted to come over to her house for coffee. She lived close to us, in the neighborhood across the street.

Kathryn, an accomplished and successful architectural historian, also semi-retired to raise her daughter, Paloma, after she married her second husband, Robert. We found out through the course of our conversation we had so much in common. We both divorced with sons from our first marriage, they were close in age, and we remarried in the same month, a week from each other. Our daughters were only two months apart! She talked to me about the joys of being a stay-at-home parent and I saw a different side of this life, a joyful one. Our friendship blossomed, and I leaned into the changes, and released the resistance which held me captive for so long.

New Path Revealed

The time arrived to allow God to tear away my layers of self-doubt and embrace the new me. I hung out with my new friends from music class and we went out to lunch. We formed a small group of parents and began gathering regularly. These times gave me so much joy. Donnie traveled extensively during this period in our marriage and the playdates served as a much-needed distraction from loneliness.

Despite feeling lost in my new world, slowly but surely my new path revealed itself to me. My friends, Val, Kathryn, and Alana offered me a joyful path to this new life waiting for me. A life of joy and acceptance of self. My **SOUL** waited to be awakened, and my **EGO's** attachment to love needed to be released. For many years, I required significance from others, and operated from fear and control. Cynthie saw me authentically. The **EGO** had darkened my path but my light emerged slowly. With God at the helm and as the light, I followed Him out of one of the darkest periods of my life.

On the home front, Donnie and I longed to build a strong foundation of faith for our family. We asked our friends for recommendations on churches. Eventually, we settled on Gateway Church, in North Austin. The conversational and relatable style of the lead pastor, John Burke, drew us in instantly. Nondenominationalism became the compromise between Donnie's Pentecostal Light faith and my Catholic upbringing. The music lifted our spirits, and the community welcomed us. The kids loved their classes, and we began our spiritual journey as a family.

As we entered our church one Sunday, they gave each of us a blank stone with a black marker and asked us to wait for John to give instructions. I remember sitting there listening to his sermon about his first years as a pastor. He described the fear and anger inside of him, and his **Desire** to experience joy. He'd lost his dad to cancer and raged against God for years. Tears sprang to my eyes, and my heart felt a flutter of emotions. I longed for the joy he spoke of and felt trapped in misery I didn't know how to free myself from. The word FREE sprung in my mind to write on my stone. My **Desire** became freedom from the fear, uncertainty, anger, resentment, and guilt...knowing the answers were deep inside of me and as I held my stone in my hand, I made a secret vow to find it within me. I sought God's guidance persistently. Every morning in my journaling practice, I spoke to Him honestly about what happened, about the fights, the betrayals. He knew my heart and could guide me better than anyone. The verse in Jeremiah 29:13, "You will seek me and find me when you seek me with all your heart" kept me focused on my relationship with myself, with Him, and my family. I sought my purpose by living it out loud daily to the best of my ability.

Embracing My Authenticity

After several months of going to Cynthie by myself, Donnie agreed to join me in counseling as a couple. He felt uneasy because he believed Cynthie sided with me about the state of the marriage. Slowly, but surely, he understood he, too, needed to let go of the pain which held him captive. She guided our communication with each other. Neither one of us listened to understand, we listened to react.

Cynthie helped me desensitize the pain from those early years with my dad, the role it played in my marriage and relationships with men, but most importantly she helped me unleash the power inside of me and tap into my intrinsic self. She guided me to rediscover my confidence by encouraging the dates I took with myself and by guiding me to Brene Brown's books that talked extensively about how my need for achievement and perfection were tied to shame and modeling from my dad.

To rediscover me, the authentic me, meant I learned how to lean into my joy. My friends, my applicability of the artist dates, my journaling practice, and most importantly, my relationship with God propelled me into a new dimension of happiness. I found out I wasn't as serious as I projected. That seriousness stemmed from my need to be responsible which resulted from the early childhood trauma with my sister. But I could choose to create a new identity of confidence, joyfulness, and serenity; my true nature. I discovered my grateful side when I began leaving small notes of gratitude for my husband and son to find. Notes that deep down provided me with immense joy because I began to see my husband in a brand new light. He became a man who loved me and our family, who provided us with security and protection. I learned that when I built a culture of appreciation in my home, everyone changed around me. Our son thoroughly enjoyed his notes even though he didn't say much about them, but years later I'd find the notes in his drawer.

Cynthie guided me to understand the power of being vulnerable and empowering others. She encouraged my compassionate side which she deemed one of my greatest gifts from God. The greatest lesson I learned was to embrace my authentic self! Be authentically me, embrace it all, even the broken parts. My creative side emerged after so many years of being dormant. God led me out of the darkest time in my personal life. I trusted the messengers He sent me along the way. We are all interconnected on earth.

Now, looking back at this time in my life, at my quest to understand why I survived in the first place, I can see God's hand in all of it. Sometimes the greatest lesson of all is to allow, accept, and stay curious. Only He knows what's coming, what lessons you must learn to prepare for when they will play out in your favor.

To live as your authentic, soulful self, seek and focus on the joy of all your experiences. Surround yourself with love, with an empowering community of family, friends, and colleagues. Initiate your conversations from a place of love, take ownership of your role in your circumstances, strive to be the best version of yourself, love with all of your heart, and love yourself. These were lessons I learned along the way on my journey to my **SOUL Identity**! Allow the energy to flow through you freely. If there's any resistance, understand it and release it. By understanding it, you will learn to acknowledge the patterns when they show up in your life because you'll understand the triggers, and what feelings show up, and **Awareness** is the first step in moving in the right direction of your life. It leads you down the path of change.

Happiness and joy exist inside of you, seek it in your everyday life. The focus is key. If you focus on what is going right in your life, on the beauty of it, the joy of simple gestures, and moments bring you then you'll see it all around you, it will grow because you are putting intention and energy behind it. Remember as Tony Robbins said, "Where focus goes, energy flows." The statement holds so much power in it because it's true.

Observe it in your life and you'll find how true the statement is. I became a negative person because of my focus, self-talk, and physical expression. These are three aspects you are in control of daily. What you focus on, how you talk to yourself, and how you carry your body is within your control. This is the programming you give your **Subconscious Mind** to create the beliefs, **Habits**, and identity that are true for you. If you **Desire** change in your life, you must understand the relationship between belief, **Habits**, and identity, and then act on them in an affirmative way.

Habits affected the dynamic in my life. It took surrendering my life to God to understand the role they played in my relationships, in my mindset, in my health, and in my career.

Scripture for Journaling, Meditation, or Prayer

Matthew 16:25 *For whoever wants to save their life will lose it, but whoever loses their life for me will find it.*

This verse is talking about surrender to God in which Jesus is teaching about losing one's life in the metaphorical sense. The interpretation I took from it was of shedding my old EGO Identity and embracing my authentic SOUL self.

Who are you called to be? What characteristics, and values define your authentic self?

Chapter 14

I Submit to God's Way of Living!

E arly in the morning in May 2017, as I furiously wrote in my journal, a prompting interrupted it.

Call Bridgett.

I met Bridgett at a career workshop my friend J. R. conducted many years before in 2011. I won a seat at Bridgett's mastermind which she led for ten weeks on the *15 Invaluable Laws of Growth* by John C. Maxwell. During those weeks, I fell in love with the Mastermind design and excelled in her ten-week course. Shortly after, she approached me to become part of the John Maxwell team. She insisted my talents in communication and connection would inspire people as a speaker, coach, and trainer. I remember being flattered by it. However, as a single mom, it made more sense for me to be part of a company that offered medical insurance and a steady paycheck. Yet the offer remained in the back of my mind throughout the years.

I asked God, "Am I to be part of the John Maxwell team?"

Yes.

His "yes" came like a feeling of butterflies fluttering throughout my body that center over my heart. I learned over time this is how God communicated His answers to my questions. To receive this answer from God is my cue to act on my **God instincts**. I called Bridgett to explain to her the prompting. As a deeply faithful woman, she understood the importance of acting on instinct and quickly set me up with Shelley, who initiated me with a profile and the onboarding process. I spoke with Donnie, who graciously agreed if it felt right for me. I needed to move forward with the process.

The certification process began a few hours later. In August 2017 and after months of taking the online courses, I flew to Orlando, Florida, and received certification as a speaker, coach, and trainer with the John Maxwell team. My dream became a reality.

A sense of higher purpose called me out of retirement. My elation quickly turned to concern. Little did I know that my decision to act on my God instinct would affect the relationships with my family. After all, for the last three years, I had devoted all my time and attention to everyone.

My interactions with Andres and Donnie became tense soon afterward. They both felt abandoned by me, yet as a coach now, I see their own patterns of behavior surface. They projected their **Limiting Beliefs** of not feeling like they were enough on me and blamed me. My son felt fearful I would revert to my old **EGO** patterns of behavior, notably the **Achiever.** My entrepreneurial venture triggered my husband's unresolved feelings from his parents' divorce.

In January 2018, I received my second signed contract to give a keynote address for the Women's Council of Realtors in Brownsville, Texas. Donnie, although thrilled initially, soon showed his true feelings.

The Enemy Remains Hidden

On a hot, dry afternoon, the weekend before my event, my husband picked a fight with me. "Aren't we enough for you? Why do you feel the need to go back to work?" His **Limiting Belief** of *I'm not enough* reared its ugly head.

"It has nothing to do with you or the kids not being enough. This is something God placed in my heart to do, and I need to obey him. Why can't you be happy for me?"

These resentments threatened to derail me from finding my **SOUL Identity**, and yet despite them, I continued on my path, the one God gave me to fulfill. I belonged to a master plan, and I finally began to grasp the meaning of loving Him first. To continue on this path to submit to God first was hard because change in social contracts can be tricky when the other spouse is in a different mind, emotional, and spiritual space than you. Despite this stress, my divine purpose and second chance at life propelled me into this new chapter in my faith journey toward my **SOUL** and divine plan.

When I began the process of obedience and **Submission** to God's master plan, I encountered my first dose of spiritual warfare. It is a concept of fighting against the work of evil spirits intent on intervening in human affairs. Only, I didn't understand what it was at the time it happened. The higher I ventured in consciousness the more I encountered and faced these distractions meant to derail my divine purpose from being fulfilled. The enemy lurked behind the scenes and used my husband's lack of belief to distract me from fully embracing this new life with joy and confidence, to deceive me by thinking Donnie didn't want me to submit to my new business, and destroy my partnership. I didn't fully comprehend why my husband, who always encouraged me to follow my dreams, suddenly shifted gears. Years later, God showed me the vile attempts by this dark spirit to stop me from shining my big bright light, and how he used my husband as his vehicle.

After the first keynote address in 2018, my work with clients kept me busy, which only deepened the resentment Donnie felt towards me. Our roles were in transition, and he fell **Victim** to the dark whispers of feeling less than and blamed me for it. When tensions and stress increase, it's best to vulnerably communicate to your spouse what your needs are in a positive way. Instead of verbally criticizing their character, utilize "I" statements and discuss your feelings to them. I needed my husband's blessing and support. My divine purpose was intertwined with his. God showed me this when His love enveloped Donnie and me in the ICU room years before. I always felt a divine connection to my husband and knew he was an integral part of my mission.

The resentment built up on both sides after five years of marriage. We lived life based on our own understanding instead of God's. Following a heated fight with Donnie in June 2018, I walked to the park adjacent to our neighborhood, sat on a bench, and begged God to help me. I desperately **Desired** to stay married. This transition from stay-at-home parent to conscious entrepreneur changed the dynamic of our relationship and the cracks showed.

A couple of days later, at my life group with other women from our church, I broke down crying with one of them after everyone left. She listened intently and, as any good friend would do, shared with me what worked in her marriage. She told me to *submit* to my husband's wants and needs. Upon hearing the word submit, it felt like someone splashed cold water on my face. **Submission** was a dirty word in my mind and something I witnessed my mom do countless times with my demanding dad. I swore I would never submit to a man's whim. In fact, I had taken it out of my vows in my first marriage and wrote my own in the second marriage, making sure I didn't include it.

Submit To My Way

Nevertheless, I stayed open to the possibility that God sent her to deliver a special message to me. During the early morning hours the next day, a prompting to leave the warmth of my bed at three in the morning woke me up.

Get up and open your bible.

My Bible is the John Maxwell Leadership Bible. He introduces each chapter in the bible with references to the Laws in Leadership. I intended to read the chapter of Jeremiah. However, I opened it to the Law of Connection, where John discussed the story of Abigail in the book of 1 Samuel.

Abigail was an emotionally intelligent wife of a foolish man named Nabal, who had infuriated David, in 1 Samuel. Upon hearing David's plans to slaughter her household, which would have included her children, she quickly gathered a feast and met up with David and with genuine humility *submitted* to David by falling at his feet and seeking his favor. The word **SUBMITTED** stared back at me! For the second time in my life, I felt God's presence all around me, reassuring me He was with me on this next journey.

I asked a simple question, "Is this what you are commanding me to do?"

The word "yes" came through clearly, followed by my question, "Why me?"

"Because you are emotionally ready and he is not."

God woke me to bring me an important message. Submit to what I am commanding you to do. Submit to living life His way (God's way) not my way.

My lesson was to accept the flow of life, stop controlling the outcomes, and live in the Now. He continued to guide me in those early morning hours. Two faces came to my **Awareness** of the coaches I researched. The faculty of the John Maxwell team encouraged their trainers, speakers, and coaches to accept coaching for themselves to ensure clarity. It is part of our development.

A particular face came into my **Awareness** and stayed there for some time.

"Is this who I am meant to work with?" I asked God.

The answer once more, "*yes,*" followed by His presence inside of me, my heart center felt a warmth, and the quickening of my heartbeat and tingling from my head to toe confirmed the choice.

The coach I picked associated herself with conditioning programs at a personal development company headquartered in Austin, Texas. I met Meshell at one of the many networking groups I attended on a monthly basis as an entrepreneur.

An Internal Battle Ensues

For days prior to this encounter with God, I prayed for strength. God asked me to submit. *Would I have the strength to do this?* My beliefs, focus, and **Habits** required change if I wanted to save my marriage to my soulmate, Donnie.

I went to bed and woke up with a newfound sense of purpose, clarity, and strength. With God by my side, guiding my every step, what could possibly happen?

This **Turning Point** gave me an immense opportunity to change my mindset. My husband often complained about my negativity. The conditioning program guided me to create a vision of the life I wanted in all categories: career, health, mindset, and relationships. I sought her help because I **Desired** to create the identity of a loving and supportive wife to Donnie, an amazing role model to my kids, an international speaker and coach, a healthier, happier me, and a positive empowered woman!

The program took me on a journey of self-discovery. The next forty-five days challenged my sanity, faith, and perseverance. I met with Meshell once a week and after about three weeks into my program, my old **EGO Identity** began testing my determination. When I introduced new changes, new beliefs, new **Habits**, my **EGO's** subconscious programming wanted to ensure I truly wanted the changes to occur, so it questioned me during those days. It referenced **EGO** feelings—I would react to them automatically.

An internal battle ensued inside of me between my **EGO Identity** and my **SOUL Identity**. My **EGO** wanted to dig in its heels and refuse to change because it felt comfortable to stay there. My **SOUL Identity Desired** to stay obedient to God's command by releasing the **EGO** and operating from love and compassion. I purposefully interrupted the **EGO** feelings to stay comfortable by creating a habit interrupt. I found that doing something physical woke up my **Conscious Mind** which helped me to stay in the present moment and deal with my feelings from a logical space. I would often leave the room to self-soothe, move away from the emotional triggers, and do something that would calm me down like take a bath or meditate.

We Were Each Other's Answers

My fear-based **EGO's** attempts to wreak havoc no longer controlled me, for God provided me with protection and guidance on how to become the wife Donnie needed me to be. When my husband experienced the changes I made to listen to him, to change my mindset to one of positivity and to stop interfering when he disciplined Andres, he began to realize that he, too, needed to contribute to the positive momentum experienced in our marriage. When my **EGO Habits** stopped and my **SOUL Identity** emerged, he saw how his flaws of being quick to anger, disrespect and lack of affection contributed to our marital problems. He felt bad, because as he stated to me one day, "I was doing all the work" and he needed to put in his share of it. Our children also felt the positive shift and responded by being more cooperative and joyful which contributed significantly to the momentum needed to emerge to my **SOUL Identity**. Eventually, Donnie decided he needed resolution and signed up for coaching.

In order to have growth-oriented relationships with others, you must decide to change first and let God step in to be your defense attorney. Only He can speak to your spouse to invoke the change needed. Believe in your higher self and your spouses' and submit to one another as you submit to God. The higher self (**SOUL Identity**) is the self that operates from love, compassion, and abundance, who is one with spirit, who gets above the noise of the outside world, and looks inward for their answers. Donnie and I felt happier than ever before. Our communication improved, and we both felt it. My habit of interrupting him improved exponentially. He felt respected and in turn, he became more affectionate with me. We gave each other grace when our flaws periodically showed up.

In September 2018, we took a trip to New York City to celebrate our wedding anniversary and attend the celebration of the life of my dear friend Nicole's dad who died months before. We had spent several Thanksgivings with Nicole and her family over the years, so Bob held a special place in our hearts. We got Mom to come and babysit Andres and Vivi. Donnie made vacation arrangements well before to alert his company of this trip. But a couple of days before, the CEO tried to guilt trip him to cancel our trip so he could travel to a job site and fix a problem with a demanding customer. Donnie stood up for us. I felt like I was first in his life. He explained he had already bought tickets to the US Open for Tennis, a bucket list item for me, and for Hamilton the musical. He told them he was not canceling anything with me and eventually the owner of the company backed him up. We spent four amazing days together, laughing, talking, hugging, kissing, and making up for lost time. We looked giddy like teenagers in love in the pictures we took of that trip.

When his cousin came to visit, he noticed a marked difference in Donnie. In the evening, after a couple of drinks, he and I had an honest conversation about our resentments and realized we were each other's answers. God united us for a divine purpose. I carried within me the answers to Donnie's prayers and he mine.

Submitting my life to God's way also affected my relationship with my dad. When I removed the veil of fear from my eyes, I saw the truth of my childhood. All the happy memories rushed to the surface. Dad did the best he could based on his own conscience **Awareness**. When you operate above the line of confusion, where **EGO** releases its hold on you, and you emerge past the illusions, lies, and **Limiting Beliefs**, your world becomes brighter and joyful. Joy is everywhere and living in the now is within your reach.

When I see or hear the word **Submission** now, there is a smile that covers my entire face. Surrendering **EGO's** hold to God allowed me to find my **SOUL Identity**.

Once you receive a taste of the life that awaits you, you do everything in your power to keep it going. This is not a one-time thing, it's continuous, and contingent on your determination to stay your course. Life will continue happening around you. You will probably lose people along the way who insist on living based on **EGO**. You will learn to discern between **EGO** and **SOUL** as you stretch your capacity in all areas of your life. Take one step at a time and know you are never alone! God's got your back like He did mine. The requirement is to step into change with faith, trust, and belief.

Scripture for Journaling, Meditation, or Prayer

Romans 12:2 *Do not conform to the pattern of this world, but be transformed by the renewing of your mind. Then you will be able to test and approve what God's will is His good and pleasing and perfect will.*

To submit to God's way meant to surrender my understanding and control of my circumstances.

Journal about a time when you fully surrendered to God's way. Reflect on the circumstances you faced, what Actions did you take, and what abundance did you receive by following His will.

Chapter 15
I Joyfully Identify with My SOUL

In December 2018, our daughter turned four, and we celebrated at home. Frank's visitation with Andres time fell on the same weekend as her birthday. Vivi called him Uncle Frank as soon as she could speak, and he took it to heart and brought her little gifts when he visited Andres. Family portraits she made sometimes included him, because she considered him part of her family and as time went on, so did we.

I spoke with Donnie about the possibility of having Frank over for her party so her brother could be with us, and he graciously agreed. We invited him for the first time to participate in a family function.

Donnie grew up in similar circumstances; his stepdad, dad, and mom grew up together and renewed their friendship, even after a bitter divorce. Donnie ensured Frank felt at home with us every time he came to our door to pick up Andres. Both being avid followers of college sports, they spoke and found a common connection through football. Their banter showed their playful and competitive natures.

Vivi's birthday arrived and true to form, Frank brought Andres with a gift for his little sister. As good hosts, we offered Frank a drink and food. When one guest dropped food on our sofa, he offered to help me clean it up. Later he asked to take a picture with both kids, and Vivi smiled widely as she sat on his lap in our kitchen. My view of my former husband morphed into a friend rather than a contentious ex.

Love changed our dynamic. Frank transformed before our eyes, and this little girl sat at the heart of it. His growth journey took him from a bitter ex-husband who believed I intentionally took his son away, often retaliating by threatening to sue us anytime the situation did not conform to his **Desires**, to becoming an active participant in family functions, and a good friend who happily co-parented our fifteen-year-old son. For the next year, our communication became friendly and open versus argumentative and closed.

Love in the Time of Coronavirus

When the Coronavirus Pandemic hit Austin, Texas, at the beginning of March 2020, Frank understood the risk both Andres and I faced with our medical history. He caringly chose to drive the six hours from South Texas to Austin to pick up our son for spring break. He knew it would expose us if he insisted on Andres flying to South Texas as the court demanded of me.

When co-parenting your kids, it's important for both parents to deal with any remnant resistance between you. Release all negative feelings to God. Donnie, my husband, modeled friendship with Frank and accepted his role in our son's life. He respected him and often told our boy how much he did to bridge the gap between us. Every experience gives you a chance to shift your focus in any relationship conflict you find yourself in. You can consciously choose to view it as a challenge or an opportunity!

Joy emerged in our household. Fear, which took full dominion over my actions for years, now sat where it belonged in the backseat. It proved beneficial when the pandemic made its grand entrance in the United States. Families were quarantined to prevent the rapid spread of an unknown assailant. Covid killed many during its rampage and continues to do so today. It changed our lives and a new normal arrived.

Restaurants closed for indoor dining, schools turned virtual, parents became teachers overnight, businesses shut down for months, highways emptied, and grocery stores ramped up their curbside pickup. Toilet paper became a scarce commodity, as did hand sanitizer and antibacterial soap. Masks evolved as the new fashion trend, and people needed to stand six feet away from others when out shopping. Humans became deprived of connection outside of their family unit. Zoom and Google Meet allowed us to reach the outside world from the comfort of our homes.

A Family of Five

To make the time pass by joyfully, we adopted a puppy from Bastrop, Texas. The kids pestered us for years to buy a dog. When my good friend Jennifer shared with me a Facebook post of adoptable dogs, we jumped at the opportunity to have a new member join our family of four. During Spring Break, we made the hour-long trek to Bastrop to find her. Vivian chose a black and white, sweet member of the pack, named Ruby, who came up to her repeatedly during our visit. We filled out paperwork that day. Andres returned a week later to help us re-name the newest member of our family, Daisy, a rat terrier, chihuahua mix. Donnie took the night shift while I woke up early to be with her. She completed our family in the most beautiful way.

Early in the morning as Daisy lay on my chest curled up as she often did during my meditation sessions, she looked deeply into my eyes, and love swelled up in me. Despite the fear surrounding us, gratitude lifted my spirits unexpectedly. In a moment of immense thankfulness, I praised God for this beautiful furry gift. As tears streamed down my face, I texted Jennifer to express my recognition of her role in securing Daisy.

Coronavirus prolonged well past the time anyone ever expected. Our family sought comfort in the love spilled during the next four months with our girl. To give Vivian a new setting, we embarked on a girls' trip to my parent's home in South Texas, where Vivi could swim in their swimming pool and enjoy the summer days. Donnie stayed with Daisy in Austin. When we returned two weeks later, we found out Donnie struggled to feed Daisy adequately, because she rejected food. Three veterinary visits later we found out our precious baby suffered from Advanced Renal Dysplasia, a genetic condition with no cure. Our girl was slowly and painfully dying. Her kidneys failed to remove the waste from her system properly. On the way to South Texas to pick up Andres after his summer visitation with Frank, we decided to end her misery.

At pick-up, Andres asked, "How's my Daisy?"

"She's not doing well, son."

"What do you mean? What happened?"

"She's dying. We have one more day with our girl. I am so sorry, Andres."

Tears welled up in his eyes, and he silently sobbed the rest of the way to Austin. When we arrived, Daisy's ears perked up at the sound of our voices. She managed to stand up slowly on the couch, where she lay lovingly curled up in Vivi's legs. The veterinarian gave Donnie painkillers for Daisy to keep her comfortable. Her tail still wagged as Andres made his way to her. It broke my heart to see her this way. My kids' dreams of having a dog gradually faded away.

Goodbye Sweet Girl

We spent the day curled up with our girl, pouring so much love and comfort her way. At dinnertime, Andres used a spoon to feed her some rice and chicken. The doctor gave us the order to give her whatever she wanted. Daisy spent the night with me, on her side, curled up in my chest like a newborn baby. If she died during the night, I did not want her to be alone.

I maintained a vigil over her the entire night and early in the morning around seven o'clock, I gave her some water. Her parched tongue welcomed the hydration with gusto. As we'd done early in the morning for the past four months, I took her outside to enjoy the sunrise together. The beautiful sunrise contradicted the way the day unfolded. We meditated in nature as tears welled up in my eyes. My heart exploded with emotions of sadness, despair, and longing for more time as the words of the guided meditation faded into my subconscious. Near the end, Daisy couldn't keep anything in her stomach. The water she drank spilled from her mouth as I caressed her head softly, telling her, "It's okay girl." She kept looking at me with a quizzical expression, almost as if she were saying, "Why can't I drink, eat, run, and play?"

Not long after, I glanced back at the house to find Andres standing by the door leading to the backyard with a deep pain evident on his face. I motioned for him to join us and, quietly, he sat down next to me and put Daisy on his lap. For an hour on a hot July morning as birds sang, we sat in a peaceful silence with our fur baby, softly caressing her ears and whispering "I love you's" to her.

The hours slowly ticked by, inching us closer to the hour Donnie would take her to the vet. One of us would be there to witness her passing over and hold her paw to reassure her. Donnie came to take her from my arms later that morning. Andres and I said our goodbyes, but Vivi didn't understand the concept of death completely. In her five-year-old mind, it meant she would see her again. Instead, she busily navigated Minecraft.

We followed Daisy and Donnie out to the car in our driveway.

Andres clung to the back window telling her, "I am here girl, it's going to be okay. I love you, thank you for being a part of our family."

I had to pry Andres physically from the car to allow Donnie the room to maneuver the car into the street.

He loudly sobbed as he yelled, "No, please don't go!"

I held my sweet boy as the gut-wrenching sobs released his body from the sorrow surging to the surface.

Free From Pain

When the clock struck ten my heart sank, for the time arrived to end Daisy's life. I prayed for Donnie, Dr. King, and for our girl. We made the loving decision to free her from the excruciating physical pain she felt for the past week. The night before, Donnie and Vivi decorated the coffin he created for her. We decided to bury her in the backyard. Although she only spent four months with our family, she would forever have a special place in our hearts.

The garage door opened suddenly and startled me. Andres and I rushed outside to find Donnie crying as he carefully placed Daisy in her decorated coffin with pink and purple hearts. She lay still and peaceful. For a precious moment, peace came over me, seeing her out of pain.

Donnie tenderly removed her collar and handed it to me, telling her, "You are free now, girl," and the three of us broke out in sobs, each taking turns to kiss her goodbye.

We envisioned spending at least ten glorious years with our dog, and yet tragedy struck and robbed us of the time we wanted with her. Grief and loss became our greatest teachers. As a parent, it was heart-wrenching to watch how Vivi gradually came to the realization that Daisy was not coming back. Days after her passing, I found her sitting on mats outside in the same spot where Daisy enjoyed the sun.

When I asked her, "What are you doing out here, baby girl?" she shrugged. "Are you missing Daisy?"

"Yes, Mommy, I am." Her chin quivered and tears spilled down her crystal blue eyes. I sat with her for an hour talking about all the silly games we played with our precious girl. Soon thereafter, she cracked up in this enormous belly laugh as she remembered all the good times gifted to us with Daisy.

Every day is an opportunity to spend it wisely. Tomorrow is never guaranteed.

Reset for Humanity

The Coronavirus pandemic interrupted my **Security Seeker** pattern, as it did for many others. It pushed me to embrace my discomfort in a whole new way. A persistent thought dominated my mind and made its way into my **Awareness**.

Write your book. It's time. Trust me.

As many in my family can attest, time turned slowly, especially after losing Daisy. Quarantine was extended in various states and families began spending all day together. With time on my hands to spare, I cultivated the ideas and stories of the book you now hold in your hands. First as a journaling exercise and then into a scheduled daily affair. The "where to start" and the "how" was up to God to figure out. My job was to act on His promptings. I learned to trust my **God Instincts**, and more importantly, act on them.

The initial months after Daisy died proved to be the hardest for me. I efficiently directed the pain into writing my book and focused my attention and love on the kids. We spent a good part of our summer in Brownsville, Texas with my parents while Donnie traveled for work. It helped to spend time with them and their dog, Chabelo. We decided it was risky to send the kids back to school and kept them virtual. Andres fell into a higher risk group with his asthma, as did I, with my history of blood clots and pulmonary embolisms. So, we spent our time at home together.

We received the gifts of time and memories from Covid. It came to reset humanity and shift it to a more connected and collaborative world. Countries began cooperating with each other to combat this unknown virus. Without the hustle and bustle of everyday life, people poured out into nature more, one of the few distractions in which we indulged. Before the virus, people hardly noticed anyone else on walks but starved for connection in their isolation, people began greeting each other and initiating conversations with their neighbors.

International and domestic travel stopped. Providers who frequently traveled for work now spent more time at home with their families. The isolation introduced connection back into our life with others, God, and self. Donnie dove into his hobby of woodworking while I wrote and discovered hiking with my kids. We ate every meal together as a family. Our bond strengthened, as I know it did for many other families. Family values resurrected. To keep our sanity in check, we began playing games together.

I Found HER

My fondest memory includes all four of us playing the "keepy uppy" game in the living room, where we attempted to keep a balloon up in the air. A game first introduced in "Bluey," a children's Disney show. Laughter and fun filled our home. Social media was filled with pictures of families eating, dancing, singing, and playing games with each other.

Covid ripped the security and certainty bandage we used to stay comfortable in our lives and reminded us, it was just an illusion our mind created to keep us safe. The fear gripped us and to cope, we conversed with God on a daily basis. He used our choices to reset humanity's lens. The focus shifted from "what's in it for me?" to "how can we do this together?" We each seized the opportunity to learn certain lessons we needed. As the days progressed into months, I could see the lesson He intended for me to learn.

Self-love enriched my life and was a necessary first step to understanding how to love God first. By doing so, I fully surrendered to His ways of living my life. The importance of following His master plan for my life became paramount. For it was a plan to prosper and to provide me with abundance and joy. The concept of it escaped me until the time of Coronavirus. Today, His insistence on writing the book makes sense. In my love for Him, I found her in my pages, the woman He created me to be. The one before the significant emotional events, trauma, **Limiting Beliefs**, **Habits**, and patterns of behavior distorted her view of life and joy. Discernment washed over me like a cool spring on a hot summer day.

Before Covid, I didn't grasp the significance of loving God first in all areas of my life. Once I did, I made loving choices that aligned to the way God loved and saw me. I learned to respect my mind, body, and **SOUL** with the influence and nutrients I gave it. I established boundaries and created win/win situations at work.

The Veil of Fear Lifted

When you know the inheritance that awaits you as God's child, you step into your divine **SOUL's** path with joy. In reflection and journaling, the answer came. God intended for me to become an author. My gift of writing showed up early in my life and continued throughout it but I didn't see it till I journeyed through my fear, into joy and surrendered, and put God first in my life.

Once the veil of fear lifted from my eyes, I discovered what He designed me to see. Beauty and joy of life are all around me. The world woke up, everything came back to life. It was as if I had been suspended in a never-ending loop in time, stuck in fear and suddenly I broke free from it. The air seemed crisper, the sun vibrant, roses filled my nostrils with their beautiful fragrance, birds sang their songs, and pauses became more pronounced as I relished all my senses. My heart swelled with each "I love you" from my kids and I found myself immersed in the now, where God lives. Memories flooded my consciousness with laughter, fun times, beautiful memories with Dad on a horse in Mexico, and my husband on anniversary trips. I kept them trapped underneath the **Limiting Beliefs**, patterns, and **Habits** of fear. The identity of a **Perfectionist** sabotaged my joy until 2020. I emerged from the darkness of fear into the light of joy and identified with my **SOUL**. The one God gave me at birth.

I moved past the noise of the outside world, intent on keeping my focus on outside distractions, and instead connected with God daily. I decluttered my mind and built my foundation on unconditional love for God, myself, and others. Joy and abundance followed. What I found to be true was that God **Desires** you to navigate life's storms with joy and belief that He will guide you to a path where you will prosper more abundantly than you can imagine. A combination of lessons learned and acting on my **God Instincts** paved my journey to **SOUL**. God was always with me every step of the way. By turning to Him in times of major transition, He guided me with His divine wisdom. I have faith and trust that my **God Instincts** will direct me, and I always have the belief that life is happening in my favor.

Most Profound Turning Point

Covid became the most profound **Turning Point** in my life. God used it to shift my focus away from the personal development company that courted my talents and interrupted my **Succeeder Pattern of Behavior**. The company led me to believe that I would lead an international branch of their brand and be part of their team. In negotiations, I realized they intended for me to give away my value for very little salary. I considered it the next big event of my life to work for them until the pandemic ended those negotiations.

The time spent in quarantine allowed me to purge the thoughts from my mind and channel them into my book in journaling sessions. The chapters came alive, and I saw myself through God's loving eyes. Courage, faith, and love spilled onto the pages with each story I wrote. He intended for me to understand my value and worth through the process of writing. One afternoon in June 2020, while I messaged Rebeca, who I hired to translate my book into Spanish, it dawned on me how my love for God and self gave me the resilience and self-confidence to navigate **Turning Points** throughout my life. I found myself in my pages, no doubt part of God's master plan all along. He became my compass and helped me steer this new chapter in my career. I used the companies as crutches to avoid the pain of failing on my own. No longer would I rely on others such as John Maxwell or this personal development company as an excuse not to create my own content. He guided me to understand my experiences were my gift to others. I found a way to transcend pain by turning to God in times of transition, stepping into uncertainty with faith, and by acting on my **God Instincts**. He led me to empower others through the stories in my book to do the same. A whole new avenue of opportunity revealed itself to me. God showed me that my masterminds, books, coaching, and values acquired through life experience are all connected with my divine purpose.

My lack of **Self-love** and need for perfection stood between me and the success. The time was never perfect for this journey to begin. It took all the doors closing for me to face why God prompted me to become a coach and speaker in the first place in 2017.

God knew this, and in reflection, the answer came. *Write the book. Trust me. It's time.*

The guest bedroom in our home became the place to write. Every morning at five, after meditation and connection with God, I rolled up my sleeves and organized my chapters.

God As My Compass

Carmen, a good friend of mine and collaborator, recommended I join writing groups led by Joyce, who helped her write and edit her award winning book on dementia. After hearing my story during a podcast interview I gave, Joyce bartered with me. I coached her through a major transition in her life in exchange for developmental editing of my book. God sent His messengers, Rebeca, Carmen, and Joyce, to help me find my way through the labyrinth of the writing world. He took care of the "how" so I could focus on the **Desire** he placed in my heart.

When writer's block threatened to derail the project, God answered abundantly through ideas. My nature walks during the pandemic served as a creative outlet to gain clarity. In journaling sessions, the answers came, and the structure of the book became clear. Soon thereafter, He prompted me to share these stories on social media, to test the ideas with the world. There were men who consistently posted comments on the stories of my book. My strategy shifted once I realized the stories didn't just resonate with women but with men as well.

With each step, my confidence and **Self-love** grew, and my need for perfectionism disappeared, along with the fear of failure. Every story revealed the answers I searched for my whole life. They were deep within me, except fear clouded and distorted them from view. Once I shredded my perfectionism, which tied itself to my **Limiting Belief** of "I am not enough" and feelings of fear of failure, I acted on His prompting to write the book. Then my **SOUL Identity** emerged from the darkness of fear. My daily self-care routine of connecting with God through meditation, writing, journaling, and exercise affirmed my **Self-love** within me, the missing piece of my life's puzzle.

In the first chapter, I shared with you the graphic demonstrating the Five Cycles of Transformation. I'm now sharing with you the graphic below that shows exactly how the events in my life proceeded through these cycles in hopes that you can apply this model to your own life. Perhaps this will help you think through how your challenges and **Turning Points** shape your identity and guide your path forward.

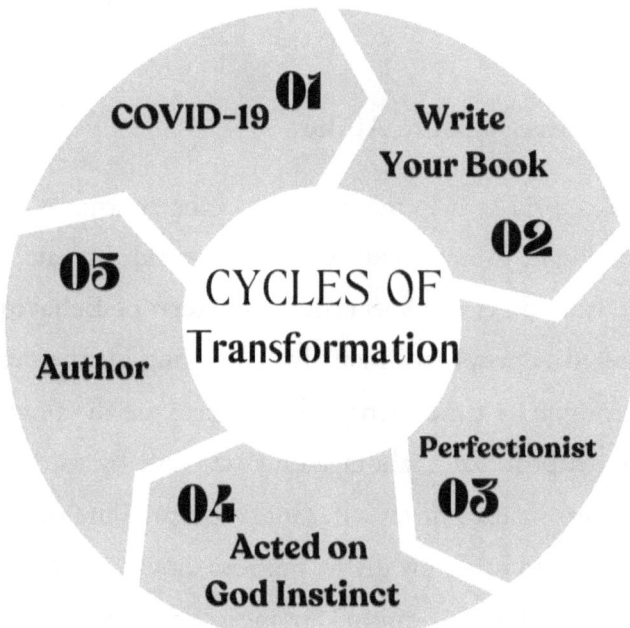

For ten years, I operated from my **EGO Identity** of **Perfectionist** and from **Limiting Beliefs** of "I am not worthy" and "Who am I to write a book to guide others," until Covid hit. It was then that I felt a strong **Desire** to write my book. At this point in my relationship with God, I learned to trust and act on my **God Instincts** which told me it was time to release my doubt and step into my divine **SOUL's** purpose. I fully emerged into my **SOUL Identity** as an author with the publication of my first book *Journey to Me: Trust the Wisdom of Change* in 2021. I joyfully identified with my **SOUL's** direction and God's master plan for my life.

From Perfectionist to Author

It took Covid to help me understand the enormous value I brought to my clients and to the world. I created a habit around being a **Succeeder**, a **Pattern of Behavior** described as people who are always looking for the next big thing. The time spent at home gave me the power to interrupt it, for I sabotaged my schedule by working for others instead of myself. God prompted me out of retirement to fulfill my divine purpose, however, my fear of failure and perfectionism kept me in a constant state of looking outside of myself for significance and worth.

I am not worthy unless I achieve.

The John Maxwell team and the growth development company represented vehicles God used to teach me valuable pieces for the book and bridge the gap in my knowledge. I acquired the experience through my transitions, and wisdom by turning inward for my answers which led me to the path to becoming an author.

The lesson in loving Him first, helped me joyfully embrace my life's plan. When I viewed my life through this lens,

I believed in myself. If He believed, loved me and saw me in this glorious light, who was I to question Him? My relationship with my husband flourished, as did my relationship with my children. My son's anxiety and OCD calmed down immensely. Dad and I laughed every time we were together.

There are gifts of imperfection I give myself daily. Anxiety and OCD no longer control me, rather, they exist peacefully in me. This intrigued my son enough to meditate daily. His OCD and anxiety calm down significantly when he incorporates it into his daily routine. By aligning with my divine purpose, I discovered that everything works out in my favor and requires less work. My joy is there for my taking, as it is for you!

My **SOUL's** journey took me down the pits of despair and back out again with the help of God's loving guidance. By staying quiet, and incorporating meditation into my daily routine, I clearly heard God's promptings and, more importantly, acted on them. This book is meant to be a love letter to all the smart, capable, empowered men and women like you who can use it as a guide to help you thrive in times of change. This world needs you to stay strong. Your light is so bright and your gifts are there for the betterment of humanity. When you surrender to God and put Him first in your life, you'll attract more abundance and joy than you ever envisioned possible.

Have courage, faith, and trust God during times of transition. **Turning Points** are life-changing. They give you an opportunity to start over in your relationship with God, yourself, and others. You receive a clean slate to shape a whole new identity for yourself, one aligned with your soulful purpose. The power to seek and find joy lies within you. I believe in you.

Scripture for Journaling, Meditation, or Prayer

2 Corinthians 5:17 *Therefore if anyone is in Christ, the new creation has come. The old has gone, the new is here!*

Reflect on a time in your life when love transformed you spiritually. Who were you before the transformation? Who did you become?

Acknowledgments

*I*n *Faith, I Thrive* is possible because of the love and care of various individuals I wish to thank. God deserves the most credit and glory. He prompted me to write the first edition of this book and patiently waited thirteen years for me to finally find the courage to do it. His promptings led me towards my divine **SOUL's** purpose as a national best-selling author, spiritual transformation coach, and keynote speaker.

Donnie, my husband, and rock, provided a loving push to launch my business and the security to live my divine **SOUL's** purpose daily. His love motivated me to step into my power and become the woman God created me to be. I'm blessed to have him as my partner in this shared mission to guide individuals to listen to their **SOUL's** promptings and live out their divine purpose with courage and faith.

My children, Andres and Vivian, emboldened me to put these raw and real stories out there in the first place. I've held the belief in my heart I'd always be a writer. As a parent, I wanted to show our children the power of following your dreams. Their pride and love for me kept me going when doubt crept up and threatened to derail my goal of being a published author.

My parents deserve a special mention. Their hard work and sacrifice also paved my path and allowed me the financial freedom to begin my work as a speaker, coach, and author. Mom has empowered me since childhood to become a writer. She always believed in my capacity and tenacity to realize my dreams. Her wisdom is shared through the thread of this book. Dad modeled grit, generosity, and grace under fire; qualities that served me well during the creation of the original work and subsequently on the second edition. I needed grit to push past my own insecurities and write about painful chapters in my life in the hopes others would feel empowered to push past their **EGO** and follow their **SOUL's** path to live a purposeful life.

I wish to thank Michelle Savage, editor of Sulit Press whose guidance gave life to the second edition of the original work, *Journey to Me: Trust the Wisdom of Change.* Her thoughtful and creative approach molded the beautiful rendition you hold in your hands today. The invaluable coaching I received from her provided me with the opportunity to improve my storytelling skills. I owe my gratitude to the team at Sulit Press, Christy Jaynes for the cover art, and Kristi Koeter for the marketing strategies that will likely result in this book reaching and impacting many lives.

To the Vixens, April Roberts, LaShelle "Shelle" Vernon, Becca "Bex" Wood Haack, Sara Heald, and Katrina Terry, thank you for keeping me accountable to finish the second edition. Your encouragement during this past year as I faced major **Turning Points** in my own life, kept me focused and motivated to live my divine purpose with conviction and power!

Lastly, thank you to the countless friends and fellow collaborators who reached out to me at the end of 2023 with texts of encouragement, prayers, and good vibes when life got tough. I am blessed to have you in my life.